Twayne's United States Authors Series

Sylvia E. Bowman, *Editor*

INDIANA UNIVERSITY

John Trumbull

JOHN TRUMBULL

By VICTOR E. GIMMESTAD

Illinois State University

 240

Twayne Publishers, Inc.   ::   New York

Library of Congress Cataloging in Publication Data

Gimmestad, Victor E
    John Trumbull.

    (Twayne's United States authors series, TUSAS 240)
    Bibliography: p.
    1. Trumbull, John, 1750-1831.
PS853.G5   811'.2   73-17016
ISBN 0-8057-0746-8

For L. G.

ABOUT THE AUTHOR

Victor E. Gimmestad did his undergraduate work at St. Olaf College, Northfield, Minnesota, and took his doctorate at the University of Wisconsin, majoring in American literature. Currently he is professor of English at Illinois State University, Normal, Illinois, and lectures in American literature and modern world literature. From 1960 to 1967 he was head of the Department of English. While on a year's leave of absence during 1968-1969, he served as chairman of the Department of English at California Lutheran College, Thousand Oaks, California. He has taught English at St. Olaf College and in high schools in Minnesota, Wisconsin, and in the Canal Zone.

Preface

John Trumbull (1750-1831), the wittiest of the "Hartford Wits," has not received much scholarly attention since Alexander Cowie's pioneering study in 1936 and the relevant sections in Leon Howard's volume in 1943. He now merits a new appraisal; for, in addition to making an enduring contribution to American letters in *The Progress of Dulness* and *M'Fingal,* he served his country with his patriotic prose and encouraged high literary standards in his contemporaries.

The present volume aims to throw new light not only on Trumbull's early work but also that after 1782, the year the completed *M'Fingal* was published. In treating his achievement as a poet and in giving emphasis to his skill in prose, it considers fresh material, particularly in light verse, political propaganda, and literary criticism. It identifies as Trumbull's some anonymous writing he did as an individual and as a collaborator—an identification made possible largely by recently discovered correspondence. Fourteen letters by Trumbull were listed by Alexander Cowie; now, including drafts and fragments, more than seventy-five are known.

Permission to quote from their manuscript holdings has been granted by the Detroit Public Library (the Burton Historical Collection); the Cornell University Library (the Moses Coit Tyler Collection); the Yale University Library (the Sterling Memorial Library and the Beinecke Rare Book and Manuscript Library); the Wadsworth Atheneum, Hartford; the Princeton University Library (the Andre deCoppet Collection of American Historical Manuscripts, Manuscripts Division); the Connecticut State Library, Hartford; the University of Virginia Library (the Clifton Waller Barrett Library); the Historical Society of Pennsylvania, Philadelphia; the New York Public Library, Astor, Lenox and Tilden Foundations (Manuscript Division); and the Connecticut Historical Society, Hartford.

Access to manuscript collections also was granted by the Huntington Library, San Marino, California, the Stanford University Library, the Houghton Library at Harvard University, the New York Historical Society in New York City, the Boston Public Library, the William L. Clements Library at the University of Michigan, and the Massachusetts Historical Society in Boston.

Other libraries which made their facilities and materials available and extended generous aid are: the University Research Library and the William Andrews Clark Memorial Library at the University of California, Los Angeles; the Morristown National Historical Park Library, Morristown, New Jersey; the Chapin Library, Williams College, Williamstown, Massachusetts; the Doheny Library, the University of Southern California; the American Antiquarian Society, Worcester, Massachusetts; the Doe Library, the University of California, Berkeley; the Hartford Public Library, Hartford; the Portland Public Library, Portland, Maine; the California Lutheran College Library, Thousand Oaks, California; the Forbes Library, Northampton, Massachusetts; the Library of Congress; the National Archives; the Milner Library, Illinois State University, Normal, Illinois; the Hamilton Library, the University of Hawaii; the Michigan State Library, Lansing; the Wilbur L. Cross Library, the University of Connecticut; the University of Illinois Library; the Michigan Historical Collections at the University of Michigan; and the Trinity College Library (the Watkinson Library), Hartford.

Quotations from letters in the Adams Papers are from the microfilm edition, by permission of the Massachusetts Historical Society.

Thanks for assistance also are owing to Dr. Samuel E. Braden, to Professor Ferman Bishop, and to Professor Sylvia E. Bowman, able editor of this series. My greatest debt has been to my wife, inspiration and co-worker.

VICTOR E. GIMMESTAD

Illinois State University

Contents

Chronology

1750   John Trumbull born in Westbury parish, Waterbury (now Watertown), Connecticut, April 24 (N.S.).

1757   Passed entrance examination at Yale in September.

1763   Entered Yale.

1767   Bachelor of Arts degree. Berkeley scholar at Yale.

1769   "Epithalamion" (published in 1789).

1769- "The Meddler."
1770

1770   "The Correspondent" (first group). *An Essay on the Use and Advantages of the Fine Arts. Delivered at the Public Commencement, in New Haven. September 12th. 1770.* Master of Arts degree.

1770- Taught school at Wethersfield.
1771

1771   *An Elegy, On the Death of Mr. Buckingham St. John, Tutor of Yale College.* Began two-year tutorship at Yale.

1772   *The Progress of Dulness, Part First: Or the Rare Adventures of Tom Brainless.*

1773   The same, second edition. *The Progress of Dulness, Part Second: Or an Essay on the Life and Character of Dick Hairbrain of Finical Memory. The Progress of Dulness, Part Third, and Last: Sometimes Called, The Progress of Coquetry, or the Adventures of Miss Harriet Simper.* "The Correspondent" (second group). "*To my good Catechist.*"

1773- Studied law with John Adams. Confidential secretary to a
1774 group of patriots.

1774   "An Elegy on the Times." Returned to New Haven.

1775   "By Thomas Gage . . . A Proclamation." *M'Fingal: A Modern Epic Poem. Canto First, or the Town-Meeting.* ["To thee, *Dear Nancy*"] (published in 1823).

1776   Marriage to Miss Sarah Hubbard on November 21. Elected treasurer of Yale on December 10.

1782   Completed and published *M'Fingal*. Resigned as treasurer of Yale.

1783   *The News-Carrier's Address to His Customers.* Letter in support of a copyright law published in the Connecticut *Courant*. Revised David Humphreys's draft of Washington's last circular letter to the governors. Helped lay the foundation for the Bar Association of Hartford County.

1784 [*The News-Carrier's*] *Address to the Gentlemen and Ladies that he supplies with the Freeman's Chronicle.* The section called "Prosody" in Part II of Noah Webster's *A Grammatical Institute of the English Language.* Hartford incorporated; Trumbull elected to the City Council, first of nine consecutive years.

1785 Collaboration on Joel Barlow's *Doctor Watts's Imitation of the Psalms of David, Corrected and Enlarged.*

1786- Collaboration on *The Anarchiad.*
1787

1789 Appointed State's Attorney for Hartford; reappointed annually until resignation in 1795.

1790 Collaborated on the "Prologue" and "Epilogue" of David Humphreys's *The Widow of Malabar.*

1791 Membership in the "Continental Society for the Promotion of Freedom," an early Abolition society. Membership in the American Academy of Arts and Sciences.

1792 Elected to the General Assembly of Connecticut. Member of the committees to build a new state house, to assist Yale, and to oppose slavery. Founder of the first Hartford bank.

1793 With Noah Webster and Chauncey Goodrich, composed the City of Hartford's address to George Washington. "The American." "Mother Carey's Chickens."

1800- Elected to the General Assembly. On committee to devise
1801 ways to perpetuate the memory of George Washington.

1801 Appointed judge of the Superior Court, first of eighteen consecutive years.

1804- Defense of Humphreys's *Miscellaneous Works.*
1805

1807 Beloved son Leverett died, age eighteen.

1808 Appointed to the Supreme Court of Errors, first of eleven consecutive years.

1809 *Biographical Sketch of the Character of Governor Trumbull.*

1818 Honorary Doctor of Laws degree, Yale.

1820 *The Poetical Works of John Trumbull, LL.D.*

1824 *Address of the Carrier of the "Connecticut Courant," to His Patrons.* Elected to Phi Beta Kappa. Honored with a dinner in New York attended by prominent literary and professional men.

1825 "Address of the Carrier of the *Connecticut Courant,* to His Patrons." First president of the Connecticut Historical Society. Departure for Detroit on September 26.

1826 Fourth-of-July address.

1831 Died on May 11, at Springwells (Detroit).

CHAPTER 1

"Strive to Build a Name"

JOHN Trumbull, born on April 24 (April 13, O.S.), 1750, in Westbury parish, Waterbury, Connecticut, had an eminently respectable heritage. His father, the Reverend John Trumbull, a member of the Trumbull family that has played a significant role in Connecticut and American history, was the first pastor of the Congregational Church in the parish, a competent Classical scholar, a practical man with extensive property, and a long-time trustee of Yale College. His mother, Sarah Whitman Trumbull, who was much better educated than most women of the time, was descended from the prominent Reverend Solomon Stoddard. From such able parentage came the prodigy who in his early years had powerful literary ambitions and who would "strive to build a name"[1] by his writing.

I *At Westbury (1750-1763)*

Both parents contributed to Trumbull's early education; but he was much in his mother's care in his childhood because he had "a very delicate and sickly constitution,"[2] as he revealed later in his "Memoir" (1820). She helped him memorize the primer and Isaac Watts's hymns for children before teaching him to read at age two. With her assistance, he read the entire Bible when he was less than four; and at that age, when he memorized all of Watts's *Horae Lyricae,* he admired the poems so much that he cried for fear that he could never equal the poetic achievement of the English clergyman.[3]

Many years later when he recalled his earliest attempt to versify, he remembered the awkward scrawl in which he wrote his four-stanza hymn and his difficulty with the first stanza:

> Come, Blessed Saviour, quickly come,
> And call a sinner to thine home,
> Where in thy bosom I may dwell,
> And in the ways of grace excell.

The last line stood thus at first.

> In knowlege of thy grace excell.

I felt, even then, the want of connection between this & the foregoing line—and after lying awake some nights, corrected it as above, by inserting the conjunction, *And*, &c.—[4]

In the years immediately following, Trumbull continued his record of precocious accomplishments. When he was six, his father, following the custom of the time, undertook to prepare for college a youth named William Southmayd. Overhearing the instruction, the son mastered more than half the Latin grammar by Lilly ere his father realized it. The parent, pleased by his son's precocity, then instructed him along with Southmayd. Young John made excellent progress, memorizing *quae genus* in one day, for example. In September 1757, when the lad was only a few months past his seventh birthday, he rode on horseback behind his father to New Haven, where he, as well as Southmayd and other candidates, was examined for admission to Yale College. As part of his preparation, he had "learnt Cordery, Tully's XII Select Orat., Virgil's Eclogues & all the Aeneid (not Georg.) & 4 Gospels in Greek." When he passed the examination, the fact was recorded in the Connecticut *Gazette* on September 24, 1757: "Among Those that appear'd to be examined for Admission was the Son of the Rev'd Mr. *Trumble* of *Waterbury*, who passed a good Examination, altho' but little more than seven Years of Age, but on Account of his Youth his Father does not intend he shall at present continue at College." Father and son rode back to Waterbury, where the child had six more years to grow and to learn before matriculating at Yale.

His achievements between 1757 and 1763 were equally spectacular. When he was eight, he read John Milton, James Thomson's *The Seasons*, one edition of *The Adventures of Telemachus* (presumably a translation of François Fénelon's *Aventures de Télémaque* [1694]), and *The Spectator*. At the same age, according to Ezra Stiles's record, he already had versified a substantial portion of the Psalms before seeing Watts's version, whereupon the talented child burned his own. Wagering at age nine that he could memorize "one of Salmon's Pater Nosters" in fifteen minutes, he astonishingly learned two of them in that time— one in Malabar and the other in Hungarian, the latter of which he could repeat to Stiles twenty-nine years later. At age thirteen he extended his knowledge of belles lettres by reading Homer, Horace, and more of Cicero. In September 1763 he again traveled to New Haven and this time commenced his long residence at Yale.

II *At Yale and Wethersfield (1763-1773)*

While at college, Trumbull experimented with a variety of poetic forms; but, because his literary remains have not come down to us intact, it is impossible to trace his development with completeness. His extant papers and his letters contain no examples of experimentation until 1765, the date of a translation from Silius Italicus. A year later two poems in heroic couplets reveal the influence of Alexander Pope. The first of these, "From a Pastoral," is a twelve-line piece praising a young man who probably was a classmate; and it possesses competent versification but no life. The second, "Introduction to a satirical poem,"[5] is an invocation to the muses that moves with vivacity and shows Trumbull at ease with the heroic couplet.

Of note also in connection with this poem is Trumbull's development as a satirist. Although we have only the brief "introduction," a modern critic has thought the poem important for evidencing an early concern with satire.[6] Relevant also is Trumbull's own statement, written late in life: "I was born the dupe of imagination. My satirical turn was not native. It was produced by the keen spirit of critical observation, operating on disappointed expectation, and avenging itself on real or fancied wrongs."[7] Supporting information is recorded in a letter by William Whitman, a Hartford friend. According to it, Trumbull once told Whitman he had resorted to satire as a defense because of "his natural excessive sensibility & feeling."[8] Trumbull's own evaluation of his nature may well be correct and could account for the fact that he began as early as age sixteen to turn toward satirical use his native gift of burlesque. This gift

had revealed itself years before "Introduction to a satirical poem,"
a fact he himself disclosed in an exchange of family information
with then Vice-President John Adams:

My mother on the contrary is a great genealogist, & has no small
share of pride of birth—She is descended from the Stoddards of
Massachusetts—but what pleased her best was that she could trace
her ancestry in the female line to a natural daughter of Charles the 2^{d}
by one of his mistresses, I think it was the Dutchess of Portsmouth.
Thus by the fashionable assistance of a little honorable unchastity
in the maternal line, I presume I have at this instant some drops of
Royal Blood flowing in my veins. From hearing this account often
repeated in my infancy, I drew up, when I was about eight years
old, & presented to my Mamma, her genealogy in burlesque; for the
impudence of which I deserved and received a good box on the ear.[9]

As far as is known, this humorous genealogy of his mother is
the earliest example of his comic talent.

As Trumbull continued his reading and his poetic experimentation, his greater aptitude in burlesque in tetrameter than for
serious or humorous verse in any other length of line became
more evident. In ["While You, my Friend, to flow'ry meads
resort"], the first of two poems from 1767 clearly indicating this
fact, he wrote in the five-stress line to an unidentified friend
about his attempt under adverse conditions "to build a name,/
And join ambitions in the chace for fame."[10] Smooth but dull,
this piece lacks the vigor and lightness found in "Poetical Inspiration." Citing as authorities Lucan and Archbishop Potter,
Trumbull described a heathen poet-priest who sat on a sacred
stool over the vent through which terrestrial exhalations
streamed, with the result that "by a *vicevers'* digestion,/ Th'
inflation rising from behind,/ It came out verse, which went
in wind."[11] Though indelicate, the poem as a whole gives evidence of a considerable talent for humorous verse of the Hudibrastic type. It is noteworthy as the first extant verse by
Trumbull that combines travesty and the octosyllabic couplet.

Of the four poems from 1768, the brief fragment beginning
["So some fair towe(r)"] is in iambic pentameter; and the three
others are in the octosyllabic couplet. Apparently feeling ebullient at the time, he enlivened these latter poems with such wit
and humor that they must have gone far toward establishing

among his fellow students his reputation for clever travesty. ["And as when Adam met his Eve"] is a slightly indecent short burlesque competently written; and "Funeral Oration" displays the talent for humorous mimicry he later developed more fully. It mocks excessive praise for deceased persons. The last portion of the poem asserts that at the death of kings "Who served the Devil all their days,/ Ten thousand bards, right wise & knowing,/ Must lend a lift, & set them going."[12] The next two lines, not published by Alexander Cowie, read, "And many a cherub coming down,/ To meet & welcome them to town."[13] For an eighteen-year-old, the poem reveals an extraordinarily sure touch in handling the subject matter and the meter. The lines move easily in the manner of Charles Churchill, and the witty gibes at the popular attitude toward death and at the eulogies given deceased persons anticipate similar ones in "The Correspondent," numbers XIV and XI, respectively.

The third poem, unusually carefree for Trumbull, is a rollicking fragment well represented by the first four lines:

> Mount "Fancy's horse," let loose the rein,
> Nor touch the pommel or the main,
> Clap spurs or strike a smarting blow,
> And Hey my lads! away we go.[14]

Whenever Trumbull "let loose the rein," he penned sparkling lines; but his goal was to write serious poems in the "sublime and pathetic" style which he presumably had seen praised in Joseph Addison's essay on Milton in the three hundred and thirty-ninth number of *The Spectator*.

If we judge from available material, Trumbull was coming into his own as a writer in 1769: not only was he writing "The Meddler" for the Boston *Chronicle*, but he also was composing verse in a variety of poetic feet. In "An Epitaph on Phinehas White, Student of Yale Col.,"[15] he achieved a smooth solemnity in a five-stress line. Although the eight-line poem has been admired both for its rhymes and its sentiment,[16] Trumbull wrote "so so" by it on the manuscript and did not include it in his *Poetical Works*. "Extempore in a dispute, On t[he] Philanthropy of the Author of Tristram Shandy," is the only anapestic poem we have by Trumbull:

When *Sterne,* who could melt at the death of a Fly,
Declar'd he was *sorry the Devil was damn'd*;
All his maudlin Admirers remurmur'd the sigh,
And the Vot'ries of soft Sentimentals exclaim'd,
"Ah! of *sweet Sensibility* this is the crown!
"What Philanthropy warm in this tender reflection!"
Not *Philanthropy,* Friends—But I'm ready to own,
'Tis a striking example of *Filial Affection.*

John 8. 44.[17]

In this short poem the ponderousness of the satire indicates
how serious Trumbull was about religion, for he had difficulty
in writing with adroit thrusts when his feelings were strongly
involved.

Far better than the preceding poem is "Epithalamion Stephani
et Hannæ," which Trumbull composed about the wedding of
the Yale tutor Stephen Mix Mitchell and Hannah Grant, who
were married in August 1769. The author established the mood
at once with his opening lines: "Ye Nine, great Daughters of
Jupiter,/ Born of one Mother at a litter." After the invocation
to the muse, he began describing the activities of the gods and
goddesses:

> *Juno* it seems, by sad mishaps,
> O'er[18] Night with *Jove* was pulling caps;
> For by this way she wont to govern,
> (So *Homer* tells) the henpeck'd sov'reign:
> But now stole off, & left him fretting,
> And rode posthaste to come to wedding.

The nymphs and birds arose, and mortals began to awaken.
The groom stood outside the bride's door and "read, or said, or
sung" a request for her to come forth. Skipping to the afternoon, the poet described the procession toward church:

> Not that more solemn (seen of old,
> As in romances we are told,
> By Hudibras, that val'rous knight)
> For joining Dog & Bear in fight.
> Nor shall we make a pause, for stating
> The odds 'twixt marriage & bearbaiting.

The guests and the clergyman, who had power to tie couples with a "gordian knot," arrived at the church; and the wedding ceremony began, the minister asking the customary questions of each and giving advice. The young couple was agreeable:

> To all the Parson said, or meant,
> Our Bride & Bridegroom gave consent.
> He bow'd & smil'd in roguish way;
> She blush'd, & curtsied, & cried, ay.

The parson pronounced them man and wife, and all returned to the bride's house for a boisterous celebration. Concluding, the poet asserted that the temblors of the wedding night presaged "something coming;/ And what that is, I'm somewhat jealous,/ A Boy will come next year to tell us."[19]

Though the "Epithalamion" may be in poor taste, Trumbull at age nineteen proved his ability to compose a lively, stimulating, humorous poem of considerable length. In doing so, he lightheartedly borrowed from the Classics; he utilized his natural skill in travesty; and he rivaled Samuel Butler in the ease with which he handled such double rhymes as "bombastic"—"Hudibrastic," "crambo"—"flambeau," "morning"—"warning," "sonorous"—"chorus," and "check first"—"breakfast." In the "Epithalamion," he reached the high watermark of his verse written while he was a student.

Tutor Mitchell felt deeply offended over the travesty by the graduate student, who, ironically enough, was later to serve with him in the legislature and on the bench. Though this poem replete with Classical allusions was a clever literary experiment, the author himself must have had some doubts about the propriety of his poem, for on his own manuscript copy he made the following note: "This Poem in the structure of it, & many particular Allusions, is designed as a burlesque on the ancient Epithalamia; particularly those of Spencer [*sic*], Claudian &c. To which we refer the learned Reader."[20] Furthermore, in his marginalia the author cited literary precedents. He insisted that Milton was more explicit about Adam and Eve; and he listed not only the general allusions to Edmund Spenser and Claudian but also specific ones to Pope, Ovid, Horace, Thomson, Shakespeare, and Milton; and he had notes on Juno and Lucina as well. The poem is filled with literary allusions, indeed, but Mr. Mitchell may have correctly thought them the less appealing part for the undergraduates, some of whom may have found it as attractive to memorize as did Asa Bacon, according to his letter to Trumbull on April 21, 1828, found in the William Woodbridge Papers, the Burton Historical Collection, Detroit Public Library. Mitchell probably took particular exception not only to his being represented as saying to his bride, "Thou'rt handsomer than all this trash,/ By full three thousand pounds in cash," but also to the ribald ending.

The poem has been published several times in slightly different forms. Cowie writes, "The 'Epithalamium' is available in its complete form only in manuscript";[21] but in June 1789 it was published in its entirety in the *Columbian Magazine, or Monthly Miscellany.* In 1805, expurgated versions were printed in the *Monthly Anthology, and Boston Review* and the *Port Folio,* and in 1855, in Evert A. and George L. Duyckinck, *Cyclopaedia of American Literature.*

For 1770, we have three poems. "Prospect of the Future Glory of America" is the peroration to Trumbull's commencement speech, *An Essay on the Use and Advantages of the Fine Arts.* After justifying in the prose section of the oration his support of the fine arts, he forecast in verse future superiority for America, which was to be "The first in letters, as the first in arms." Alluding frequently to belles lettres, he called for more attention to it in the colleges and prophesied for America authors the equal of Jonathan Swift, Addison, and Shakespeare. All in all, he succeeded better with the prose than with the verse, which consisted of heroic couplets filled with eighteenth-century poetic clichés. The two other poems for the year are "The Speech of Proteus to Aristaeus"[22] and ["Join too the hooting Owl in chorus"].[23] The first, a translation from Virgil's *Georgics,* tells in iambic pentameter the story of Orpheus and Eurydice. The other, a short, rollicking piece comparing poetry to a cathartic, illustrates again Trumbull's ease in the eight-syllable line.

After being granted a master's degree in 1770, Trumbull spent a year in Wethersfield. When scholars have speculated about what he did during his stay there, most have inclined to the view that he taught school, possibly because the anthologist Elihu Hubbard Smith said he recalled "that Mr. Trumbull was engaged in the business of instruction"[24] at one time. But conclusive evidence that Trumbull was a schoolmaster lies in his own reference to being a "pedagogue" when a friend sent him a copy of Oliver Goldsmith's description of a schoolmaster in *The Deserted Village* a few months after that poem was published in 1770.[25]

It seems likely that at least six of the eight manuscript poems dated 1771 were written in Wethersfield before Trumbull's return to New Haven. A fragment included among the six was composed in January as part of the verse epistles Trumbull and David Humphreys sent each other. Genial and lively, it said the author was sending a few lines despite the fact that "Winter's frost ('tis said) at once/ Congeals a Genius to a Dunce."[26] Unfortunately, the page containing the remainder of this jolly, sprightly poem is missing. Some of the verse from this year was merely experimental. On March 10, 1771, Trumbull wrote "[Th]e Village Merchant" in the manner of *The Deserted Village,* a fact obvious in the opening:

> Beside that untrod way, with grass run o'er,
> The Village-Merchant kept his little store.
> To gold his mind by strong attraction drew,
> Not the touch'd needle to the Pole so true;
> Though young in life, he wondrous skill display'd,
> Knew all the rules, & all the tricks of Trade.[27]

The poem fails for lack of a point, but it does display adequate handling of the five-stress line. An imitation presumably intended to be jocular is the "Elegy on the death of a Sheriff," a "Parody on Gray's Elegy in a Country Churchyard." The poem, dated August 20, 1771, contains quatrains such as the following one, which does not succeed either as serious or as humorous verse:

> Full many a gem of purest ray serene
> The ocean's dark unfathom'd caves contain;
> Full many a rogue must play his pranks unseen,
> And waste his mischiefs on the vulgar train.[28]

Also unsuccessful was a poem from July of the same year, "Advice to Ladies of a certain Age,"[29] which Cowie speculates may have arisen from the same incident as the "[E]pistle [Address]s[ed] to Mr I. J." This poem, however, was written in July 1771, some months before the occasion leading to the other. In both of them, the verse lacks the light tone appropriate to the subject, possibly because Trumbull was too close to the persons and problems involved.

When his good friend Buckingham St. John drowned on May 5, 1771, during a sea voyage from New Haven to Norwalk, Trumbull attempted different verse forms for a commemorative poem and decided on that of Thomas Gray's famous "Elegy." He felt the loss deeply and wrote in a solemn and restrained mood, as the first stanza reveals:

> The world now yields to night's returning sway,
> The deeper gloom leads on the solemn hour,
> And calls my steps, beneath the moon's pale ray,
> To roam in sadness on the sea-beat shore.[30]

The poem was printed as a broadside in New Haven in May 1771, and it was published with an introductory note in the Connecticut *Courant* in April 1772.

In December, after returning to Yale as a tutor, Trumbull composed the elegy "On the Vanity of Youthful Expectations." Once again copying the stanzaic form of Gray's "Elegy," he turned out a piece of verse which was capably done but which had a hollow ring, for when he wrote, "Hence, gaudy Flattery, with thy siren song,"[31] the thought in the poem was at odds with the author's ambition to achieve fame.

Trumbull's difficulty in combining his rapierlike thrusts with the five-stress line is clear in "[E]pistle [Addres]s[ed] to Mr I. J." The record shows that Miss Sally Perrin of Wethersfield, aided by a strong deposition from Trumbull, won a case against Mr. Isaac Jones of New Haven for slander.[32] In the pentameter poem, written from the viewpoint of Sally and attacking Jones as a liar and villain, the savage indignation is not tightly controlled or effective. Near the end, Sally predicted "vengeance":

> . . . I have friends, whom interest cannot sway,
> Thy pride dishearten or thy threats dismay;
> The time shall come, to clear my injured fame,
> And teach thee, falsehood is the road to shame.[33]

The flagrant attempt to denigrate Sally seems to have appalled Trumbull, with the result that his righteous anger over the affair lingered.[34]

In 1772, Trumbull's poetry again was marked by diversity of subject and meter. In this year he published Part I of *The Progress of Dulness,* a work which is discussed in another chapter. ["The Muse now mourns in sad, repentant verse"],[35] an eighty-line poem he did not publish, appears to be an autobiographical account of a mood of discouragement motivated by his opponents' onslaughts. Though the poem lacks the spontaneity and liveliness of those in tetrameter, it is valuable for its barbs aimed at John Vardill, a Loyalist writer, and for its reflection of the mood of the author. From the mention of fops and dunces, it appears that at least the first two parts of *The Progress of Dulness* were completed and that the reaction to Part I may have discouraged him temporarily in his quest for poetic fame.

A better poem is "The Owl and the Sparrow. A Fable" that reflects the influence of John Gay, Butler,[36] and Churchill. In a note, Trumbull explained the occasion for the verses: "In the course of a poetical correspondence with a friend, having received a very humorous letter in ridicule of Love, &c. I sent him this fable in return." Trumbull opened the fable with the idea that all animals could speak in the old days and avowed that they were not limited to prose, as "Each Bullfrog croak'd in loud bombastic,/ Each Monkey chatter'd Hudibrastic." A sparrow going to an owl for advice on love received doleful anti-female sentiments. After the owl's pessimistic speech, the poem concludes with a jocular reference to David Humphreys, whose name was represented by asterisks:

> Thus Owls in every age have said,
> Since our first parent-owl was made;
> Thus Pope, and Swift, to prove their sense,
> Shall sing, some twenty ages hence;
> Then shall a man of little fame,
> One ***** ********* sing the same.[37]

More mature than the "Epithalamion" and more smoothly flowing, this poem proved that its author had reached the proficiency in humorous verse incorporated in *The Progress of Dulness* and *M'Fingal.*

In 1773, Trumbull's literary productivity remained at a high level. Not only did he publish parts II and III of *The Progress of Dulness* and about two-thirds of the thirty essays in "The Correspondent," but he also wrote several poems. After visiting Boston in the spring or early summer, he decided to spend a year in the law office of John Adams in that city. Announcing his crucial decision to become a lawyer, in "Epistle to" (probably Humphreys) he said that he bade "Farewell to every muse's theme,/ To every soft poetic dream" and then turned his "looks with deepest awe,/ Toward Sages learned in the law."[38] The remainder of the light, facile, jaunty poem records some of Trumbull's reflections on the legal profession.

Less amusing was "On the Marriage of Two special Friends of the Author, Mr D. L. and Miss S. C.," an eight-line poem containing no geniality. In it Trumbull made scornful remarks about both the evangelist George Whitefield and the couple, Daniel Lyman and Statira Camp. Trumbull dates this poem as 1769, but Cowie points out that the marriage occurred on November 15, 1773.[39]

III *At Boston* (1773-1774)

While Trumbull was in Boston, he devoted some of his time to writing verse. One result, the serious "An Elegy on the Times,"[40] is discussed in Chapter Four. Another example of his poetic activity there, "To a Lady on returning her thimble," exhibits the author's skill in using tetrameter in light verse after the manner of Matthew Prior in his "Epistle to Fleetwood Shepard, Esq." After mocking popery and mentioning religious relics and lovers' mementoes, Trumbull concludes:

> Nor is it right you should recall it;
> I justly stole it to retaliate;
> For sure you'll own, or must dissemble,
> My heart at least was worth a thimble.[41]

It may be that in this poem, possibly influenced by Pope's *The Rape of the Lock*, Trumbull was thinking of a lady in Boston; but two letters by him make it seem more likely that he had in mind one of the young girls in Stamford.[42]

The two remaining poems from 1773 were included in the *Poetical Works*. The "Ode to Sleep," influenced by "L'Allegro" and "Il Penseroso," is perhaps the best of his poems in a serious vein and the most personal. Dated only "1773," it probably was composed in Boston, as the seventh stanza is written from the point of view of a lover separated from his beloved, here indicated by five asterisks [Sarah]. The first of ten sections is as follows:

> Come, gentle sleep!
> Balm of my wounds and softener of my woes,
> And lull my weary heart in sweet repose,
> And bid my sadden'd soul forget to weep,
> And close the tearful eye;
> While dewy eve with solemn sweep,
> Hath drawn her fleecy mantle o'er the sky,
> And chaced afar, adown th' ethereal way,
> The din of bustling care and gaudy eye of day.[43]

In 1776 the poem was altered by the addition of a section in which he paid a heartfelt tribute to his friend and former fellow tutor, the Reverend Joseph Howe, who had died in 1775. Though influenced by Milton's poems, the ode lacks their simplicity and easy grace. It repels modern readers with the numerous personifications and the relentless inclusion of adjectives. But judged according to the standards of the day, it was superior.

"The Prophecy of Balaam," a biblical paraphrase written in December 1773, seems to show the influence of Watts and to have many indebtednesses to Gray's *Bard*.[44] It may reflect the author's association with Howe, who was serving a church in Boston during the time Trumbull was there. Less readable today than the "Ode to Sleep," the poem contains more of the stereotyped diction and personifications common to much eighteenth-century verse.

The rest of the extant serious poems composed in Boston are among the least attractive by Trumbull. In January 1774 he wrote "The Destruction of Babylon: An Imitation,"[45] a paraphrase of passages in Isaiah and Revelation. The poem is undistinguished verse in iambic pentameter couplets. "On some Ladies joining to hiss M^r Q———'s oration at the Commencement at Harvard College"[46] heavy-handedly expresses strong antagonism toward opponents of the Quincys, Boston friends of his.

The remaining lighter poems are far superior to the preceding serious ones. "To a Young Lady, Who requested the Writer to draw her Character. A Fable"[47] is a graceful refusal to make the attempt. Using the congenial octosyllabic couplet, Trumbull compared "the Fair" to clouds in their changeability, clouds which even an expert artist could not capture because of their constant alterations.

An example of the type of thing Trumbull might have excelled in had not the war begun and turned his talents in a different direction was a clever parody dated "Boston 1774" in which he purportedly advertised a book to be called "Poems on Several Occasions; Part first—designed as a specimen of about three thousand Volumes of the same species of poetry, composed by the Author & others." Promising a volume of light verse, the author offered to produce poetry for any occasion; and he added a jolly postscript: "N.B. He also composes riddles, rebuses, anagrams & acrostics, for the use of the Ladies only. No kiss, no Acrostic. Beware of Counterfeits, for such are abroad."[48]

Although some have thought that no poems written for the volume have survived,[49] at least two did. The first of them, "To a Lady, who made the Author a present of an Embroidered Purse," is a charming piece with a consistent tone. Representative of the forty-eight lines are the following:

> When first your present gay appear'd
> I doubted, wonder'd, look'd & stared,
> Nor guess'd what moved my Fair to send
> A Purse to her Poetic Friend.
> . . . .
>
> And those are wise, by Reason strongest,
> Who send such Gifts as last the longest;
> While You, the wisest far of all,
> Send gifts I cannot use at all.[50]

Both the swift turns of thought and the dancing movement of the lines indicate that light verse was congenial to Trumbull. The same qualities are found in "The Ring," an eighty-eight-line piece, which has fewer deft touches but is nevertheless an amusing, fanciful toying with the subject. The two poems are strong evidence that had Trumbull developed his talent for light verse, he might well have contributed distinguished examples to the type. As it was, he rarely utilized this talent, probably because he, like many of his American contemporaries, thought such verse inferior.

IV *At New Haven* (1774-1777)

In 1775 Trumbull wrote the first portion of *M'Fingal,* which is discussed in another chapter, and "To my Friends, Mess.ʳˢ Dwight & Barlow. On the projected publication of their Poems in London." In the second poem Trumbull addressed his friends, "Pleased with the vision of a deathless name,/ You seek perhaps a flowery road to fame"; and he warned them that hostility to their work could be expected. Reflecting, perhaps, the warfare over the worth of colonial literature, as well as his opposition to condescending British literary critics, he forecast that the reaction in London would be unfavorable; but he advised his friends to go ahead, foreseeing that "Fame shall assent, and future years admire/ Barlow's strong flight, and Dwight's Homeric fire."[51] In this estimate of his friends' poetic abilities he was, of course, greatly mistaken.

Only a few other poems remain from this period. Some are mediocre epigrams, such as "Vox Populi, Vox Dei" (1776);[52] but more appealing is ["To thee, *Dear Nancy*"], a piece of humorous verse which was printed (presumably as Trumbull had written it) in the *Independent Statesman & Maine Republican* in 1823. An introductory note told that in 1775 Trumbull had composed a poem of sixty-eight lines to assist a bashful associate named Thomas Wooster in his courtship of Miss Nancy Cook:

> To thee, *Dear Nancy,* thee my sweeting
> Poor Colonel Thomas sendeth greeting.
> Whereas, so pleas'd the powers above,
> I'm fallen most desperately in love;
> For Cupid took a station sly,
> In one bright corner of your eye,
> And from his bow let fly a dart,
> Which miss'd my ribs, and pierc'd my heart;

> Pierc'd through and through, and passing further
> Put all my insides out of order.[53]

The remainder of the poem is full of exaggerated protestations of Thomas's love, and a last line that threatens suicide upon refusal by Nancy. Like "The Purse" and "The Ring," composed in Boston earlier, this poem produces in the reader a sense of Trumbull's potential in light verse.

Not always recognized in the twentieth century as Trumbull's, ["To thee, *Dear Nancy*"] was known as his by his contemporaries. Cowie does not mention it, but Leon Howard lists it as "a transcript of an item in the *Detroit Gazette* for October 3, 1823, supposedly taken from the *Portland* (Maine) *Statesman* and including about seventy lines beginning 'To thee dear Nancy, thee my sweeting.' "[54] Apparently circulated in manuscript among Trumbull's friends, it was alluded to by Mason Fitch Cogswell in some doggerel in which the poet prays that a bullet, like the dart of Trumbull, might " 'miss his ribs & reach his heart/ And piercing through & passing further/ Put all his insides out of order.' "[55] The poem seems not to have been published before 1823, although Noah Webster printed a much altered version in the *Impartial Gazetteer, and Saturday Evening's Post* on Saturday, July 5, 1788 (No. 8). He made numerous rewordings, added thirty-two lines, and used the name Jacob instead of Thomas, possibly because Thomas Wooster was still living. He did not attribute the poem to Trumbull at the time, but in his *Manuscript Bibliography of the Writings of N. Webster By Himself*, he made the specific identification in his own handwriting: "J. Trumbull's Love Letter for Thomas Wooster. Impartial Gazeteer [*sic*], July 5, 1788."[56] The *American Mercury*, the Connecticut *Courant*'s rival in Hartford, printed "Jacob to Nancy" on August 25 of the same year (V, 216), and a reply called "Nancy to Jacob" a week later (V, 217). In 1804, the *Port Folio* printed "A Poetical Letter: From Lovesick Jacob to Coy Nancy" with an introductory note: "[From the manuscript stores of a friend and amateur, we derive the following. It has strong resemblance to the lively and caustic style of John Trumbull, Esq. If the author of M'Fingal woos in such a mode as this, every muse, if not every maid, ought to be propitious.]"[57] Then nineteen years later what appears to be the original version was printed in Portland, Maine. It was copied by the Connecticut *Journal* on August 12, 1823 (LVI, 2911) and by the Detroit *Gazette* on October 3, 1823; and it may have been printed in other periodicals as well.

Experimenting with verse forms popular during the eighteenth century, Trumbull attempted the ode, the elegy, the translation, the verse fable, and the biblical paraphrase. Although he tried the anapest at least once, he favored the iamb. He was adequate in pentameter, but he excelled in tetrameter. He read widely in English literature and obviously was influenced mainly by Milton, Pope, Gay, Gray, Prior, Swift, Churchill, and Goldsmith. In the "Epithalamion," he illustrated his broadening Classical knowledge and his improving skill in travesty. By and large, he was not successful in serious poetry except for "An Elegy, on the Death of Mr. Buckingham St. John" and the "Ode to Sleep," both of which are merely competent.

This survey of the early poems by Trumbull which are known gives us a fairly clear idea of his development as a minor poet. Beginning with his introduction to Watts under the tutelage of his mother, he became acquainted with Greek, Latin, and some English poetry while he still was very young. At an early age he also began his attempts at versification; unfortunately, of these experiments only one stanza of one hymn remains. In New Haven during his college years and in Boston, he developed into maturity as a poet. He demonstrated that he had a gift for light verse and burlesque, that he had ability in satire, and that he found the octosyllabic couplet the most congenial verse form.

CHAPTER 2

"Trial of His Genius"

THE privately circulated "Epithalamion" was a literary mile-
stone for Trumbull. Written when he had what he later
characterized as a "Flow of Vivacity & Spirits,"[1] it heralded the
arrival of his mature poetic style; and it immediately preceded
his most prolific period. From 1769 to 1773, when he still had
strong ambitions to become a professional author, he composed
not only his portions of "The Meddler" and "The Correspondent" but also the unpublished "Speculative Essays," an uncom-
pleted novel called "The Mathematical Metaphysician," and *The
Progress of Dulness*. Except for the school year 1770-1771, when
he taught at Wethersfield, he was at Yale during this period
as a third-year graduate student in 1769 and as a tutor for the
last two years.

I *"The Meddler"*

Trumbull made the first known "trial of his genius" with the
essay series "The Meddler" when he was nineteen and his
associate, Timothy Dwight,[2] was seventeen. Their work was
printed in the Boston *Chronicle*,[3] the first essay appearing in the
issue of September 4-7, 1769, and the last in that of January
18-22, 1770. Apparently they sent several essays or perhaps all
of them to Boston at the very beginning; for John Mein, one of
the publishers, added a note at the end of the first explaining
that the others would be delayed because space was lacking.

It has been suggested that Trumbull brought the series to a
close of his own choice,[4] but another explanation for the dis-
continuance of "The Meddler" seems equally valid. When Mein
returned to England in November 1769,[5] he left the material
on hand for his partner, John Fleeming, to print. It may be

that the Boston men were ready to publish what they already had but sent word that they wanted no more. If they did, such action would account just as satisfactorily for the fact that Number X ends with the promise of a different fare for the next week as does the idea that the young authors stopped sending material.

A comparison of the printed version of "The Meddler" with the manuscript reveals numerous changes, most of them minor, such as the reversal of order from "great merit & genius" in the manuscript to"great genius and merit" in the published version. Occasionally words were substituted, transitions smoothed, and faults in parallelism corrected. In some instances, sentences which may have seemed unnecessary or offensive were struck out. Evidently the material was at times rearranged, for two parts of V in the manuscript are printed in III. More important were the omissions, as, for example, the following passage from VIII: "Every satire, replied Mr. *Freeman*, is liable to misconstruction from the ignorant, the tasteless & the malicious. There are always a set of men, who will not allow the corruptions of religion to be ridiculed. From these I should expect nothing else, but that they would infer (since I laugh at their austerity of habit & affectation of behaviour) that I would advise a preacher to dress in a suit of regimentals, to enter the pulpit with a cockade & feather in his hat, & take his text & doctrine out of Hudibras, or the Earl of Rochester." Whether Trumbull or the editors struck the passage is not certain. The action, though, may have been fortunate because comparable statements appearing later in "The Correspondent" drew enraged denunciations.

In the work on "The Meddler," Trumbull and his collaborator made unequal contributions. Trumbull had the overall responsibility and furnished six and two-thirds of the numbers; Dwight wrote three and one-third. The former introduced the series (I) and wrote on wit and humor (II); flattery (III); a coquette (III); "words, points and signs" (V); pseudo-scientific essays (V); the degeneration of the world and contemporary vices (VII); enthusiasm and affectation in religion (VIII); and Milton and several other topics (X). Dwight wrote about politeness (IV), biblical poetry (VI), and the education of children (IX); and he included poetry in two numbers (III and VI).

The choice of subjects is consonant with Trumbull's own view of the differences between the natures of Dwight and himself. In his description of the "little society" producing "The Meddler," he characterized the members as he saw them. The group consisted of John Manly, Esq., Mr. Thomas Freeman, Jack Dapperwit ("descended from the famous *Tom Dapperwit,* formerly celebrated in the *Spectator*"), and a clergyman. Manly (Dwight) is pictured as gentlemanly and serious, little given to humor and satire. Freeman (Trumbull) is an accurate self-portrait: "In his character, he is a great humourist, has an odd and peculiar way of thinking, and a ready discernment of every thing ridiculous, in writings, actions or conversation: but at the same time is a great admirer of every thing that is/ just and beautiful. He is a friend to sincerity and plaindealing and consequently an enemy to all kinds of affectation and hypocrisy, which he never fails to lash with satyrical indignation." The descriptions harmonize with the estimates of the two men by later generations.

The styles and the choice of authors from whom mottoes were derived also differentiate the work of the young friends. Dwight drew his mottoes from Horace, Ovid, and Cicero; and Trumbull took lines not only from Horace and Virgil but also from the satirists Persius and Juvenal. Dwight was consistently serious and solemn, as in his opening sentences in IX: "Nothing contributes more to the pleasure of parents, the advantage of their families and the good of their country, than a faithful discharge of their duty in the education of their children. Thoughts on this subject, and the good and ill consequences arising from the faithful, or unfaithful discharge of it shall be the subject of the following paper." Though Trumbull agreed with such sentiments, he employed a style in his own work that contrasts markedly with Dwight's, for he gives a sense of playfulness, exuberance, and boldness to it, some of which is satirical. These characteristics of Trumbull's writing are evident in the various quotations in the pages following.

The young men wrote in the tradition which was established by the enormously prestigious Richard Steele and Joseph Addison in the *Spectator,* the *Tatler,* and the *Guardian* (Steele). Trumbull, who had been familiar with the *Spectator* from age eight,[6] and his associate presumably read the bound volumes of these periodicals, which were listed by President Thomas

Clap in *A Catalogue of the Most Valuable Books in the Library of Yale College* (1755). Though verse had dominated Trumbull's notebook, he had enough confidence in his prose to write, after the manner of Steele and Addison, for publication as an essayist. It is in relationship to their overwhelmingly influential example that "The Meddler" needs to be considered.

The indebtedness of the two colonial teenagers to the British essayists was predictably great. In addition to the major borrowings in form and content were the many smaller ones such as the use of mottoes, letters, Latin names, a club, and poetry. The title may have derived from references in the *Spectator* to the *Medley*, an anti-Tory weekly, or from Addison's description of the Spectator in the first issue as one who had lived "without ever medling with any Practical Part in Life."[7] Furthermore, a title connoting mischievousness may have been suggested by the name *Tatler*. Whether the young men appropriated the strong moral tone from the British is uncertain, for they would have stressed morality under any circumstances. When they included diverse subject matter, as in the third, fifth, and tenth "Meddler," they seem to follow the pattern of the *Tatler;* but generally they appear closer to the *Spectator*, especially in its individual motto for each number, its literary criticism, and the initials at the end of each article.

Most of the mottoes for the ten numbers of "The Meddler" apparently were the authors' own, but some duplication of those in the British series existed. "The Meddler" II and the *Spectator* 51 use the same motto: *Torquet ab obscaenia jam nunc sermonibus Aurem* (Horace, *Epistles*, 2. 1. 127). The motto of VI is half that for the *Tatler*, 108.[8] *Nostri en farrago libelli!* in X overlaps the most conspicuously because not only does the *Spectator* use "*farrago libelli*" in 609, but the *Tatler* in the folio issue employs the following for the first forty numbers and for several later ones: *Quicquid agunt homines . . . nostri farrago libelli* (Juvenal, *Satires*, I, 85, 86). Both kinship with Steele and Addison and obligation to them seem clear from such use of mottoes.

There were also some dissimilarities between "The Meddler" and its English patterns. In their short series the young collegians had no Bickerstaff or Sir Roger de Coverley, though they did have a "Schemer." They employed only one initial for each

author (*B* for Trumbull and *E* for Dwight); and Trumbull in-
dulged in parody and in one instance slyly alluded to his partner's attempts at the sublime in verse. But the greatest difference
was in tone, for the students lacked the sophistication of the Eng-
lishmen, who were thirty-nine at the time they began the *Spectator*. Like other imitators, the youths were unable to achieve
the genial urbanity with which Addison in particular censured
follies and vices.

Trumbull remained closer to his British models in some of
his essays than in others. Among those in which he departed
least were I, II, and part of X. In these numbers, he often drew
hints from scattered parts of the *Tatler* and the *Spectator* and
incorporated them in one essay. When he explained his aim
in the initial "Meddler," for example, he could look to the *Tatler*
for the idea that polite persons "may be instructed, after their
reading, what to think" (1, Steele); and he knew the goals of
the *Spectator* "to admonish the World" (4, Steele), "to enliven
Morality with Wit, and to temper Wit with Morality" (10,
Addison), and "to banish Vice and Ignorance out of the Terri-
tories of *Great Britain*," and "to establish among [the British]
a Taste of polite Writing" (58, Addison). In his appraisal of
writing, furthermore, he could emulate Addison's avowed intention to attack the crime rather than the individual (16). Stating
his design, Trumbull promised a variety of subjects treated in
a moral, nonpartisan, and impersonal manner. Perhaps less
humbly than his English predecessors, he announced his aim of
"instructing the unlearned, diverting and improving the learned,
rectifying the taste and manners of the times, and cultivating
the fine arts in this land." Though this goal for a brief series
may have been too lofty, the language in which it was couched
was commendably vigorous, direct, and graceful.

In the tenth "Meddler" Trumbull again seems quite close to
the English journalists when in his potpourri he notes the hours
kept in town by some gentlemen. At ease with long sentences
and parallel structure, he writes to his country readers:

I will therefore tell them . . . that by the encouragement and assistance
of people in great towns, the afternoon has of late behaved itself
very unbecomingly, made great encroachments upon his neighbours,
and strangely justled and discomposed the other parts of the day;

it has driven forward the morning from its proper station, and forced it to take refuge in the habitation of noon; it has made breakfast and dinner shake hands, and has been the total destruction of supper; it has devoured a large portion of night, and, unless a speedy stop be put to its motion, may probably swallow up the whole four and twenty hours.

For this passage Trumbull may well have borrowed ideas not only from Steele in the *Tatler* (263) and Addison in the *Spectator* (317 and 323) but also from Swift's *Journal to Stella*, in the last of which the dean writes of dining at four and at five. The problem of the afternoon, we suspect, was more likely to be found in London than in colonial New Haven.

In the second "Meddler," another of his more derivative numbers, Trumbull revealed how near he sometimes remained to his sources and how he tended to be more caustic than Addison. Adopting ideas from the extended discussions of wit and humor found in the *Spectator* (numbers 35, 58-63, and 422), Trumbull argued that "True Wit depends upon genius and nature, the false upon labour or affectation"; and he condemned the anagram, the acrostic, the rebus, unintelligible talking, raillery, and the double entendre, just as Steele and Addison had. Trumbull himself acknowledged his closeness to the *Spectator* when he mentioned several kinds of false wit which had been "justly ridiculed by Mr. Addison," one type being the rebus. In number 59 Addison, drawing upon William Camden's *Remains Concerning Britain*, had described the rebus in a leisurely and genial manner, referring to Classical examples such as Caesar and Cicero, and to a more recent one in England: "Mr. *Newberry*, to represent his Name by a Picture, hung up at his Door the Sign of a Yew-tree, that had several Berries upon it, and in the midst of them a great golden *N* hung upon a Bough of the Tree, which by the help of a little false Spelling made up the word *N-ew-berry*."

In the printed version of "The Meddler" Trumbull merely lamented the existence of "a new kind of Vermin, begotten between the Anagram and Riddle, called the *Rebus* which is the most pure, refined and sublimated kind of nonsense, that has appeared in any age. . . . I shall let them pass as proper play things, for the diversion of fools." But in the manuscript version he discloses the close link in his mind of Addison, rebus, and

Newberry by a sentence immediately following the word "fools": "They are the toys & rattles of children six feet high, to whom Mr. Newberry has [ingeniously enough] dedicated one of his little collections of puerile verses."

In several other essays Trumbull adhered less closely to his exemplars. Though the influence of Steele and of Addison was present, it dominated his writing to a smaller extent and served mainly to provide material which he cleverly adapted. In the third "Meddler" he modified the idea of a "tatler" or "spectator" and arrived at a "schemer." This character offered his services as a flatterer who had written what he thought "the quintessence of panegyric, and the marrow of dedication" as a result of studying "the poetical addresses of Dryden, the odes of Monsieur Bouileau [*sic*] in praise of the French King, and the writings of the whole herd of moneyless poets."

In the same "Meddler" he seems to have modified the substance on a coquette in the *Tatler* (27) and the *Spectator* (281) and on inventories found in the *Tatler* (42, 113, and 216), the last of which ended with an advertisement. In the *Spectator* (281) the coquette's dissected heart reportedly rose in a glass tube "at the Approach of a Plume of Feathers, an embroidered Coat, or a Pair of fringed Gloves." Altering the various ideas he found in his reading, Trumbull created an advertisement listing the property a coquette wished to sell before her impending marriage. The inventory included "several bundles of darts and arrows, which are well pointed, and capable of doing great execution, a considerable quantity of patches, paint, brushes and cosmetics, for plaistering, painting and white washing the face; and several dozens of *Cupids*, with all their appurtenancies, very proper to be stationed on a *ruby lip*, a *diamond eye*, or a *roseate cheek*." While not completely original, the "schemer" and the advertisement for the coquette were skillful, intelligent adaptations which were a credit to their author.

Numbers X and V also contain examples of the modification of ideas. In the first of these, there is the term "Political Arithmetic," which in the *Spectator* (200) had been applied to an economic discussion concerning the basis of wealth. In "The Meddler" the same term is used, but the application is made to moral problems and to criminal justice. Arguing that the nobility was exempt from penalties under the law, Trumbull contended that under his system of "Political Arithmetic" "the title exactly counterbalances the crime." In the printed version it is not evident that the author was referring to specific cases, but in the manuscript Trumbull specifically stated in a note that he was referring to Lord Baltimore and Sir Francis Bernard. And in V he may have utilized Addison's essay on the cat-call, a type of whistle (*Spectator*, 361), as a burlesque on "trifling projectors" writing pompously on inconsequential subjects. Mimicking the work of these "projectors," Trumbull stated that he had "composed several very learned treatises upon the comma, semicolon, period &c., and upon the signs of admiration and interrogation," and he contended that there was a need for more printed signs and for training people to register the proper emotion for each. Though in these essays he lacked the easy good humor of his illustrious predecessors, he at least displayed his talent for borrowing technique and for altering ideas to suit his own intentions.

The burlesque of the "projectors" was effective enough, but even better was that in the same "Meddler" on the speculations of those inventing ingenious but improbable explanations of nature's mysteries. Trumbull may have been affected by Steele's and Addison's gentle jokes about the Royal Society in the *Tatler*; and, if he saw the mocking essays on the same group in *Useful Transactions in Philosophy*, he may have received hints on method. Whatever the influence, the result was zestful, exuberant exaggeration in a paper on madness. Trumbull's purported author contended that ideas must "swarm out" of the skull for lack of space and ordinarily escape by the tongue or fingertips. But, if the usual routes for escape are blocked, the ideas "presently begin to swell, foam and ferment and press prodigiously against the skull; till with pushing by each other, fighting for place, crouding, squeezing, and mixing with the brain, they breed such uproar and sedition in the head, that the patient cannot chuse but to fall into fits of raving and delirium, which after some continuance terminate in settled and downright madness." To conclude on a light note this effervescent description of insanity, Trumbull had his author recommend trepanning to let out an excess of ideas and promise to send his servant with a drill to operate upon mad writers, religious enthusiasts, and lovers he knew.

In several numbers Trumbull displayed less dependence on his models and even differed with them. In X, containing his best work in the lighter vein, he made observations about the circumbendibus, some modern poets, and Milton, comments which are included in the chapter on literary criticism. In VII and VIII, he revealed especially well both strengths and propensities. In VII, he possibly drew his initial impulse from scattered comments Addison made about the relationship between the ancients and the moderns. Addison had found the ancients superior in some respects, such as good sense. Trumbull, who departed from Addison's view, deftly used the idea of the degeneration of the world as the starting point for an ironic condemnation of modern foibles and vices, working in a parody on the style of James Hervey as part of it. There is no specific attribution in the printed version, but in the manuscript Trumbull made an asterisk and commented, "From hence this paragraph is a parody on the affected pomp of style, we find in the celebrated *Hervey's* meditations." Repudiating the view that the world had degenerated from an original perfection, he declared first that he had seen no one who would admit he himself was not so wise as his forebears, and, second, he did not think the opinion had a sound basis. Then, with the ingenious use of irony, he attacked social evils and foibles by arguing for superiority in politeness, dancing, exaggerated compliments, cursing, drinking, gaming, poetry (the lowest qualification of a gentleman), fighting, and dying.

Reflecting an essay by Steele in the *Spectator* (478), the author averred that France had "long enough been called the kingdom of politeness, and been allowed to enjoy the monopoly and sole manufacture of oaths, curses, compliments and fashions"; and, probably inspired by Addison's academy for women in the use of the fan (*Spectator*, 102) or his academy for politics (305), Trumbull proposed that two universities be built in all centers of population: one for gentlemen, one for tailors. No one should be allowed to make the nobility's suits who did not possess a doctorate; and in the college for gentlemen there would be additional staff members to teach not only dancing, fencing, and gambling but also swearing. This resourceful spoof is the best specimen in "The Meddler" of its author's graceful style, his adeptness in irony and parody, and his moral commitment.

Number VIII is distinguished by Trumbull's direct attack on "Enthusiasm and affectation in religion" and by his defense of satire, both topics of great immediate interest to him. In the *Spectator*, Addison had made scattered references both to enthusiasm and to doleful countenances. For example, in 201, he had termed enthusiasm and superstition "two great Errors"; in 407, he referred to "the Bellowings and Distortions of Enthusiasm"; in 494, he called Sombrius one "of these Sons of Sorrow." Addison was outspoken in his condemnation of religious fanaticism, but Trumbull exceeded him in vigor and frankness; and he was more explicit in censuring pretense.

In doing so, he employed the device of a rough draft of a letter Mr. Freeman supposedly had written some years earlier. The requisite qualifications in it for a clergyman were mockingly stated as grace or hypocrisy, a somber expression, and a sizable "grey Wig." Maintaining that half the "modern Saints" looked grave as owls, the purported author said Sombrius could serve as a pattern for the type because of his unusually sober appearance. And accompanying gravity should be arrogance and impudence. Armed with them, a clergyman could vaunt his own religious life in public, ask anyone whether he had been converted, and tell saints from sinners. The results, Freeman asserted, favored the zealots: "Indeed this will greatly disgust the learned and polite; but what of that? They make but a small part of the world: and the vulgar will readily believe your assertions, flock together to hear your discourses, stun your ears with the din of their praise and raise you to a level with the Old Prophets and Apostles." Thus through a fictional letter did Trumbull sting sharply the more aggressive disciples of the Great Awakening, ones whom he would soon excoriate at greater length in "The Correspondent" and in his notebook.

When the clergyman in the group objected that persons guilty of extravagant behavior were treated too ludicrously in the letter, the author spoke through the character of Manly to make his first clear and explicit defense of satire as a respectable literary method which could be used against enthusiasm and affectation. To begin with, Manly condemned enthusiasm as dangerous. Though it admittedly was less objectionable "than open depravity," it yielded equal or worse results because "The villain disgraces himself only; the enthusiast disgraces religion:

the one is an open enemy, the other a private traitor." Then he supported his method further by contending that mockery is best suited to the subject and is more likely to benefit mankind, including his targets, because "satire strikes at the root, by shew-ing the man of affectation that the conduct by which he hoped to gain applause has subjected him to ridicule and contempt." Citing Addison, Manly argued that wit should be an ally of truth rather than a foe; and he expressed a wish that someone as able as the English essayist might arise to champion virtue, fight vice, expose minor social ills, scourge more serious ones, and support the golden mean. Through Manly, then, Trumbull cogently defended satire, drawing on the immense prestige of Addison in so doing.

Trumbull's first venture into print has almost been forgotten. Howard has characterized the series as "sprightly, readable, and mildly amusing."[9] Cowie has said, "Exceedingly apt in expression, they want sufficient originality and power to carry them very far on the road to posterity."[10] To be sure, they are derivative as well as lacking in the urbane and tolerant spirit found in the English models; but they reveal courage, careful observation, youthful ebullience, skill in sentence movement, competence in the use of satire, and acquaintance with Classical and English literature. The essays by Trumbull approached the "Augustan manner of smooth clarity and easy firmness"[11] found in the *Tatler* and the *Spectator*. There is, furthermore, a sense of mastery in the imitations and adaptations, and the best exam-ples are the incisive irony in VII and the bold attack on excessive religious zeal in VIII. As a production aimed at "the worthy and judicious part of mankind, whose esteem only is worth our pursuit" (I), they deserve respect; and, as the first "trial" (I) of the author's genius as an essayist, they were a success.

II *"The Correspondent"*

Less than a month after "The Meddler" ended in the Boston *Chronicle*, Trumbull, again assisted by Dwight, began "The Correspondent" in the *Connecticut Journal, and the New-Haven Post-Boy*.[12] His apprenticeship served in the Boston series, he was prepared for a more extensive publishing venture, one in which he was to employ his talents more freely. Literate, knowledgeable, and courageous, he was still only nineteen when the first essay was published on February 23, 1770.

"The Correspondent" differed markedly from "The Meddler." The essays were concerned with subjects much nearer to the colonial readers, they were much less derivative, and they more closely followed their author's nature and interests. Only rarely did mottoes head the contributions, and initials at the end of numbers, with one exception, were abandoned in favor of an occasional "Amicus" or "Saulus." There were several collabora-tors, some of whose identities have not been established. And "The Correspondent" appeared in two different sets: the initial eight, from February to July, 1770; IX through XXXVIII, from February to September, 1773. In the first instance, Trumbull discontinued the series because he was departing for Wethers-field, and in the second he ended "The Correspondent" because he was leaving for Boston to study law with John Adams.

The first set of "The Correspondent," written entirely by Trum-bull and extant in his hand except for III by Dwight, was limited to a few topics. In I and II, Trumbull announced his intentions; in four numbers (IV-VII), he satirized some contemporary metaphysicians; in VIII, he contributed a searing indictment of slavery. All seven essays he wrote are marked by serious purpose, mordant satire, and skillful prose. He stressed instruction, with the result that the characteristic emphasis is moral earnestness, a fact to be expected from the young author's announcement in the first one. Although his avowed ethical intent may well have seemed commendable to his readers, the use of ridicule may not have; for he thought it necessary to defend his proposed use of it in rooting out social ills. But being firm, confident, and militant, he made satire his chief weapon.

In opening his series, Trumbull told his readers what his plans were for it. After explaining his title by reference to the popularity of letter writing in his day, he offered to be "an universal Correspondent" (I) and promised a nonpartisan ap-proach and a combination of instruction and amusement. As he put it, "though I may sometimes attempt to divert and entertain you, [I] shall make it my principal aim to assist you in distinguishing between your friends and enemies." He in-sisted, furthermore, that the best friend should point out certain faults and errors to save others from harm; and, acting in such a capacity, he vowed on the one hand to expose some undeserving persons that the world held in high esteem and, on the other, to defend the world against the small group that held it to be wicked and growing more degenerate.

Well aware of the contemporary colonial prejudice against the satirical mode, Trumbull also justified its use in treating these and other topics by pleading its efficacy and by sharply distinguishing between the role of the satirist and that of the slanderer. As an example of the latter, he named Xantippus, who used the mask of religion to hide his malicious talk (II). Trumbull disclaimed any attempt at a merely rhetorical exercise when he said he would "be very sorry to draw a character that would hit nobody's likeness," and he asked only that the reader apply it to himself before he applied it to his neighbors. Anticipating hostile reactions, he countered them by cleverly warning that "the bird that flutters is certainly known to be wounded."

He indicated more clearly the controversial nature of his subject when, after opening his second essay with a light touch concerning critics, he listed a few prospective titles. In doing so, he resorted to the device of "a curious set of manuscripts" written by "a departed Author" and that person's friends. These men supposedly had written about many subjects, including oratory, dancing, quarreling, and the art of achieving worldly position. But more significant were those bearing on religion, for they had a direct application to the theological climate of the time in Connecticut. One was "The Art of Second sight . . . first invented by a renowned Stage-player, and since brought to perfection by the united labours of a certain set of Philosophers"; and another was "Creeds and Catechisms made and mended; by D. D. and Company: being the substance of many treatises that have lately made a noise in the world." The printed version does not identify the characters, but the manuscript contains notes marking the famous English revivalist Whitefield as the "Stage-player" and the Reverend Joseph Bellamy as "D. D." Most important of these topics was "A New System of Logic," for it was the only one on which Trumbull actually wrote.

The fact that a nineteen-year-old student would devote four articles to the current ecclesiastical strife may seem strange, but his doing so is indicative of the religious furor accompanying the Great Awakening. Among the leaders in the vitriolic exchanges were some of Jonathan Edwards's disciples, men who seemed indefatigable in the skirmishes. Describing the quarrels, Trumbull wrote in his notebook, "Every Pamphlet, every Newspaper was filled with metaphysics; the press groaned with controversy; & the world was stunned with Sermons, Letters of debate, Replies & Rejoinders, Dialogues between Ministers & Parishioners, & such like weapons of this spiritual warfare, whose names it would tire one to reckon up."[13] That his picture was accurate is attested to by the articles and advertisements in the newspapers. In the Connecticut *Journal* on December 2, 1768, for example, a letter defended the Reverend Samuel Hopkins against the censure made in the paper on November 4. On December 30, a letter signed "The Querist" raised objections to the letter of December 2 and asked three questions concerning it. In the same issue there was an advertisement for *A Dialogue, between a Minister, and his Parishioner, concerning the Half-Way-Covenant*. Many more letters appeared in this newspaper alone.

Concerned over ecclesiastical debate which had run into excesses, Trumbull pioneered in Connecticut the use of satire to silence religious argumentation, as he himself stated in his manuscript notes some years later: "And I have the honour of being the first, who dared by Satire to oppose the party of controversial Scribblers, & set this part of America an example of the use of Ridicule & Humour, to combat the whims of dogmatical Enthusiasts, & expose the extravagance of that foolish ambition, which would extend our reason beyond the bounds of revelation."[14] A modern critic has agreed that this approach was new and, incidentally, added the complimentary observation that "laughter produced by irony, not caricature, is a step nearer to real art."[15] The defense of satire, together with the list of possible topics and the announced serious purpose, gave promise of writings with a sharp edge rather than a graceful vapidity.

With the two introductory essays out of the way, Trumbull applied dexterous satire to the problems most on his mind. Being greatly concerned over the disputatious metaphysicians and their mathematical style of reasoning, he fired his first salvos at their stronghold, reason, with deftness and skill. Combining the approach of the Scottish school of common sense with the irony of Swift, he attacked it as their "New System of Logic" (IV). This structure, he argued, had as its "two grand pillars" the following ideas: "1. That the common sense and reason of mankind is so weak and fallacious a guide, that its dictates ought never to be regarded"; and "2. That nevertheless there is nothing so great that it can surpass, or so perplexing that it can entangle the understanding of a true metaphysician." Then he quoted "an ancient fabulist" as deriding "fruitless enquiries, concerning things that lie beyond the limits, which God and nature have set to our knowlege," and blamed an unenlightened age for the fabulist's opinions. "A great enmity," the author maintained, "hath in all ages subsisted between metaphysics and Common Sense." Whether the readers agreed with Trumbull's ideas or not, he had defined the issues with precision and clarity.

In the succeeding columns, Trumbull put even more bite into his style by adding burlesque and parody to his ironic utterances. He asserted, for instance, that the divines lacked sufficient technical terms and then suggested a remedy: "A few *Entities, Quiddities, Quinta-essentia's* and *Esse-reale's* would make a most becoming figure to deck with Italic characters a page of metaphysical reasoning, or strike nobly on the ear, when thundering from the mouth of a controversial dialogist" (VI). And he added a mock book advertisement parodying the style used for the volumes by them:

Now in the Press
and will speedily be published,
A Vindication of true Religion,
Being an answer to the remarks of
The Revd. Dunscotus:

Wherein is shewn, that the remarker hath wholly mistaken the nature of the subject, and that he hath been guilty of the most palpable blunders and absurdities: Concluding with a catalogue of his contradictions, and an appendix, proving the coincidence of his opinions with those of *Hobbs, Spinoza* and the Atheists and Deists in all ages.

Given Trumbull's acumen and boldness, the implication in the reference to Duns Scotus is obvious. He brought the issue of proofs into sharp focus with the following contention: "For if our tenets are not conformable to the scriptures, we must by some

means force the scriptures to become conformable to them."
And, with deliberate incongruity, he advocated that metaphysicians be preferred to the Gospel for spiritual guidance.

He further mocked them and their arguments by means of a
humorous imitation of their dialogue style (VII). In making his
points, he raised his queries through an "Objector," who in one
part of the dialogue questioned whether any good would come
from such controversy. The metaphysician answered, "The argument fairly stated stands thus: Truth sometimes breeds contention; therefore whatever breeds contention is truth." After record-
ing a number of such exchanges, Trumbull expressed hope for
an imminent answer to "Whether there be any such thing as
matter?" as well as to many other abstruse questions.

After thorough castigation and exposure of their weaknesses
by Trumbull, the metaphysicians responded with oral rather than
printed denunciations of the Correspondent. Though their sensi-
bilities were bruised, perhaps they realized the justice of the
strictures at the same time as they resented them; and they
may have sensed that the Correspondent's ideas were approved
by a public weary of the contentiousness revealed in some of
their spiritual leaders.

Taking leave finally of these particular opponents, Trumbull
turned in the eighth and last essay in 1770 to the evil of slavery.
Here again he used Swiftian irony, perhaps a little less savage
than that in *A Modest Proposal* but powerful nevertheless. He
applied it to those advocates of slavery who quoted the Bible to
the effect that the meek (Americans) shall inherit the earth and
who argued that much labor was expended to teach the Negroes
Christianity. Sardonically, he offered as proof "constant assertions, that this is our sole motive" for enslaving them and the
fact that he himself had "heard of no less than three, who know
half the letters of the alphabet, and have made considerable
advances in the Lord's prayer and catechism." In a final sarcastic stroke at sanctimonious defenders of slavery, he concluded
with a proposal for sending vessels "to fetch off the Pope and
the Grand Signior" for the religious instruction of those two
church dignitaries. The method he used was very effective in
destroying the moral pretensions of those who cited altruism
or Scripture as a defense of slavery. Though this publication is
not one of the great documents in the war against involuntary

servitude, it is one of the earlier; and it is of enough significance to be discussed and reprinted in the *Journal of Negro History*.[16]

The first series, now ended, clearly demonstrated both Trumbull's ability to handle mordant irony and his disposition to exploit its potential when his feelings were aroused. By holding his opponents up to ridicule he may have performed a needed service, but he seems to have made more enemies than friends. Perhaps it was fortunate for him that, upon leaving New Haven for a busy new job, he discontinued "The Correspondent," an action which he recorded in his manuscript as contrary to the advice of his friends.

On February 12, 1773,[17] Trumbull resumed the series, announcing his aims and bringing the work into its contemporary context. He desired, he said, "to furnish . . . an entertaining series of miscellaneous essays," banning "no subject, or style, that is not dull, low, or grossly personal." After alluding to the angry reception given by some readers to the earlier group, he characterized the time as a "mild interval from the struggles of patriotism and self-interest" and as one "of liberty, while the praise of home manufactures is not yet quite forgotten." Somewhat slyly, he ended with a tongue-in-cheek observation that potential contributors could scarcely delay writing when they considered how much the world desired advice and profited from it.

The thirty essays appearing in 1773 indeed qualified as "entertaining." Trumbull's contributors wrote on industry and application, the desire for money, the governance of private families, charity, learning and pride, quacks, friends, flattery, and a coxcomb. Of these, only the last was in verse. Generally they dealt with fairly innocuous subjects, that on quacks excepted. In the approximately two-thirds of "The Correspondent" which he himself wrote, according to his notebook in the Moses Coit Tyler Collection, the Cornell University Library, Trumbull was far less pacific, except for the list of aphorisms or the single disquisitions on public spirit and on eulogies for the dead. When he wrote on his main topics of ignorance and dullness, hypocrisy, slander, and quacks, he engaged in a spirited and bitter fight with a variety of antagonists.

The three more conventional numbers are utterly disparate in subject matter, style, and value. All of them display their author's gift for neat phrasing and crisp endings, often with an unexpected twist; but there is little other similarity. As might be expected, the group of aphorisms treats many subjects, as can be seen in the following examples: "A little wit, like a little courage, is always seeking occasions to display itself"; "He, who affects to despise mankind, shews not their meanness, but his own superlative pride"; and "The greatest earthly happiness consists principally in the delusions of the imagination" (XXV). These aphorisms appear to be the unpolished expressions of a keen observer, and they probably were hurriedly composed because of the pressure from his trip to Boston about this time. All in all, this article probably is Trumbull's weakest in the entire series; and the sayings represent a slight performance compared with Benjamin Franklin's *Sayings of Poor Richard*.

The essay on public spirit (XVI), probably influenced by Silas Deane in Wethersfield, strikes a different note from all the others. Two and a half years earlier in his commencement oration Trumbull had lauded patriotism, and now, in the spring of 1773, he was praising the earlier resistance to the Stamp Act and regretting the loss of continued patriotic interest. Although he was fundamentally a conservative, he went so far at this time as to write that "tho' mobs are always hurtful to the community in their immediate actions, they are sometimes very advantageous in their consequences." His main point, however, was that "not one in twenty" knew the significance of the Writs of Assistance and that "no body seems to feel the least concern for the danger of our privileges." Direct and lucid, this essay was the only one in which the Correspondent discussed politics and treated a subject without humor, satire, or obvious strong feeling.

In XI, the best of his single essays, Trumbull parodied eulogies containing overblown praise, an act consistent with his lifelong opposition to affectation. In the introduction to his elegy on St. John, he had attacked excessive tributes; and, in the elegy itself, he had followed his own advice. Now in 1773 he condemned the current eulogies not only by emphatic statement but also by a burlesque of them. He averred that one found it "difficult to distinguish an honest man from a knave, or a wise man from a fool; for the old maxim of saying nothing but good of the dead is construed to extend to telling lies in their favour." As an example, he included a purported flowery eulogy, part of which read as follows: "And at last, full of days and full of honours, when, with *Caesar*, he had lived long enough both for nature and glory, to the unspeakable loss of his bereaved friends and his weeping country, this Glory of Sextons, this Flower of School-committees, this Ornament of Corporals, and Phoenix of Cobbles [*sic*] was snatched away by relentless Death, in the 81st year of his age." As a specimen of Trumbull's demand for sincerity and his proficiency in burlesque, XI ranks high.

All the rest of Trumbull's contributions to "The Correspondent" in 1773 were facets of the bitter controversy in which he became embroiled. The main reasons for this situation were the connection with his other writings, the treatment of his subjects, his own nature, and his theory of satire. First, "The Correspondent" of 1770 and the current *The Progress of Dulness* were powerful irritants to some readers. The connection with the first of these was made by the author himself in the very first number (IX) of the series with a reference to "some Persons of eminence" who three years earlier had irately "called the Author, all the *rogues, rascals, knaves* and *scoundrels,* that could be invented...." In a sense, this association made the fight a renewal, an intensification, and an extension of that in 1770. And the fact that Trumbull was the author of both the newspaper series and *The Progress of Dulness* must have been suspected by many.

Second, in Trumbull's day people expected serious subjects such as religion to be treated with gravity, certainly never with scorn or humor. Third, the nature of the author was fearless and what today would be called feisty. And, fourth, was Trumbull's view of the function of satire. He opposed the personal type except in three cases: (1) to defend oneself against injury; (2) to champion "injured innocence"; and (3) to protect the public from a man whose vices have become harmful to the general welfare (XXVIII). He did not advocate satire for its own sake but as a last resort: "When any being has arrived to a certain pass of wickedness, no motive will influence him but Shame; they, who despise Virtue, are afraid of Contempt and disgrace, and those who would turn a deaf ear to the calls of Reason, are often checked by the arrows of Satire" (XXIX). Clearly, when he aimed at holding transgressors up to mockery and shaming them into better behavior, he trod on many toes. Furthermore, in his intense earnestness, he was closer to Swift and to Juvenal than to writers such as Addison.

With passing months the attacks on Trumbull grew in frequency and strength. As early as March, a reference appeared to carping criticism (XIII); in May, "Philiatros" charged in the Connecticut *Journal* that the Correspondent was "a universal genius" writing only for the amusement of "mankind" and for his "own vanity"; and, on June 25 (XXVIII), Trumbull reported threats of physical violence to the Correspondent: "He is to be assaulted in private, caned, kicked and cudgelled; he is to have his nose cut off, his eyes knocked out, and his head beaten to a mummy; besides which, he is to be hanged, tarred and feathered, with several other punishments. . . ." On July 16, L. H. reported a sarcastic request from "a very large and wise council of ministers convened at Westminster" for rules on admission of candidates to the ministry. Two weeks later, L. H. sent a more lengthy caustic letter, this time accusing the Correspondent of self-importance and, by implication from a biblical quotation, of "childish" writings.

It must have been about this time that some anonymous versifier composed the following doggerel:

> On reading the Pamphlet entitled "The Correspondent"
>
> Why dost thou thus of other slanders rage,
> When thy own slanders glow on every page?
> Why dost thou thus on *Decency* declaim,
> When thy foul pen betrays thy want of shame?
> Why dost thou thus on *Truth* say things so grave,
> When thy own *Falsehood* mark the faithless knave?
> Why thus the *Christian Pastor's* province tell,
> When thy own writings shew the *Infidel?*
> Be either *good,* or *bad,* and stop such evil,
> Nor take an *Angel's* form to serve the *Devil.*

These lines presumably were circulated privately, as they can be found in the Cogswell Papers but not in the Connecticut *Journal.*

On August 6, "Boltrope" shrewdly placed a mock advertisement listing *"materials for fabricating Essays, Songs, Sonnets, Odes, Elegys, Orations, Satires and Lampoons,"* stating, in a gibe at Trumbull's five feet four inches, that the goods were on

"the small bark, Correspondent, Hector Bluff, *Commander."*
A week later, L. H. in a long letter denied that he himself was a
clergyman and asked for proof that dullards were admitted to
the ministry. Then on August 20, Boltrope, acting on the Correspondent's announced demise, with vitriolic ingenuity first charged
his opponent with owning a "valuable stock of Arrogance, Impudence and Impertinence" and then included a tombstone inscription concluding:

> He fell,
> A Victim to a lingering Disorder, resembling
> a Catarrh, or dripping of the Brains,
> And died of an empty Scull,
> In the Tenth Year of his Age——Anno Dom.——

A fictitious letter by "Tim Grocer" in the same issue implied that
the Correspondent was himself a "coxcomb." On August 27, "Observer" warned the Correspondent to use more moderation; and
"Fusee," in the one defense of Trumbull, warned Boltrope not to
attempt matching wits with the Correspondent. Finally, on September 3 Trumbull's opponents attacked in numbers. "Twig" contributed some doggerel mistakenly accusing the Correspondent of
following David Hume, but Boltrope and "Moderatus" did better.
The former addressed a note to Fusee charging the Correspondent
with "arrogance and presumption." But Moderatus struck the
cleverest blow of all. Obviously countering Trumbull's use of
Egyptian mythology in the story of Theuth, Moderatus likened
the Correspondent to the ichneumon, which he said kills croc-
odiles by crawling into their bellies and then gnawing out
through their sides. Moderatus drew the following lesson:
"Herein the Correspondent and Ichneumon seem to act from the
same disinterested motives. The Ichneumon receives no benefit
from his labours; and it should seem as if Mr. Correspondent
had very little hopes of doing any good by his essays." With
these three blows, Trumbull's enemies made their most intensive
onslaught in the battle, which ended abruptly with his departure
for Boston.

In this affair Trumbull proved himself a powerful disputant.
He was well acquainted with the Classics, mythology, legends,
religion, English literature, and the Bible. He had at his command both supple prose and jocular verse. He employed figures

of speech only rarely; but he frequently used analogy, example, burlesque, and irony. He began his columns with vigor, and ended them with a sharp, powerful stroke. He had great tactical skill, putting his adversaries on the defensive constantly. At the time they accused him of infidelity, for instance, he praised the clergy, pointed to danger from Deism, and insisted on the need for higher standards for entrance into the ministry.

When the attacks on him became heavy, he printed in July a verse letter (XXXII) Humphreys had sent him in February which foretold the rise of enemies, and next in a verse answer he (XXXIII) lightly dismissed the arguments. With a variation of the many proverbs about knaves and fools, he ended, "While fools and knaves are nine in ten,/ We'll pass for wits and honest men." After L. H. sent letters to the newspaper, Trumbull replied with an essay on letter writing (XXXIV), concluding with a scathing example of a satirical epistle addressed to L. H., in which he refuted with acuity the shallow contention that the Correspondent was an enemy of the clergy because he spoke the truth to them.

But Trumbull not only had the skills, he had moral courage, a quality which Mark Twain reminds us is rare in mankind. As Trumbull himself stated, he wanted the ability to make himself heard, the strength to expose "riot and extravagance, and that spirit, which can equally despise and defy, the insulting terror of open threats, or the more dangerous meanness of secret malignity" (XXVIII). With his literary ability and his character traits, he was a match for his opposition.

The first group of essays constituting the controversy in which he was engaged is the one concerning hypocrisy, affectation, lying, defamation, and slander—all of them representing a departure from the frankness, sincerity, and truth which he prized. Of the three, two (XIII and XVIII) presumably involved a private dispute, previously referred to, concerning Miss Sally Perrin. In the first, Trumbull accomplished his purpose through a pretended letter castigating two characters drawn in the manner of La Bruyère. He portrayed Sombrio as a lugubrious seeker of a reputation for piety and Malicio as the liar and slanderer who, in his attempt to build up his own reputation by destroying that of others, sat like a spider grinning over the remains of his victims. This essay seems somewhat caustic, but

XVIII was even more so. In his staunch support of Miss Perrin, he pilloried lies and ended with scornful derision more effective than his "Epistle to Mr I. J.":

> Then shall thou wish, turn'd out to grass,
> To truck conditions with an ass;
> Or since in thee like temper's found,
> To crawl, a muckworm, in the ground;
> Nor find, amid that ten-legg'd rabble,
> An animal so despicable.

In the third (XXX) essay of this group, Trumbull was concerned not with a single enemy but with a substantial portion of the clergy. He trod dangerous ground when he asserted that "there is no vice more detrimental to the world than Hypocrisy," but he drew blood with the following charge: "In every class, that is graduated, some of the best scholars and a great part of the worst undertake the work of the ministry. And such is the tenderness of examinations, that the worst pass as smoothly and become as reverend as the best." Next he put the clergy on the defensive by maintaining that "Deism, Prophaneness and Profligacy" had recently been making great inroads. Despite the strong compliments paid to the ministers in the beginning paragraphs, the implied linking of hypocrisy with a number of them was provocative. The strong verbal attacks on Trumbull resulting testified that some pastors would rather vilify and misrepresent him than correct their faults—and that they were much more offended by the exposure of hypocrisy than by its practice. As ridicule, the essay was commendable; as a tactic for improving the ministry, it was disastrous, for proof could hardly be given.

Of those subjects connected with the disputes, ignorance and dullness are the ones most closely linked to his other publication of the time, *The Progress of Dulness*—indeed, they may serve as companion pieces to the first two parts of that poem. While in *The Progress of Dulness* Trumbull made his points through simple, declaratory statement, in these two essays he made them through the device of Egyptian mythology referred to in the *Phaedrus*. According to the Correspondent, the Egyptian god Theuth had given mankind the arts and sciences but had had to provide "counterfeit amusements" for the ignorant and dull.

Only at the end of XXII did Trumbull use irony, when Theuth told "his intimate friends and acquaintance . . . it never entered into his thoughts, that any man who had any share of common sense, or any abilities for higher pursuits, would" fall prey to vices. In the next issue, Trumbull condemned fools through an imaginary prophetic speech by Theuth, one full of biblical echoes, proclaiming the future ascendancy of coxcombs and fools in a time when learning would be despised. As weapons in the battle against the critics of *The Progress of Dulness,* the Egyptian mythology and the fictitious prophecy were clever and entertaining.

Later (XXIX), he continued his war on folly and dullness by allegory. In an adroit stroke, he referred to his source as one from which John Bunyan had drawn hints. According to the purported allegory, the arts and sciences march from west to east with Sense and Genius first, Fancy and Invention next, and Humour and Satire last. Applying the comparison to America, he argued that, although religious "enthusiasm" was nearly defunct, there were many serious faults and evils in the colonies and that "a thousand inferior Daemons of Foppery, Riot, Lewdness, Luxury, Cheating, Lying, and Prophaneness" were both "numerous, and prevalent." According to the Correspondent, Humour and Satire were a last resort against these multiple examples of folly and dullness.

In several numbers of "The Correspondent" opposing quacks and mountebanks, Trumbull depended largely upon forceful statement and apt phrasing to win his argument. Today his attack possesses mainly historical interest, but in its era it may have helped raise the standards of medical treatment. One of the ideas he had was to link the etymology of mountebank with the account of a prisoner hanged from a cart the preceding summer (XXVII). Another was to conclude with the witty remark that the problem of quacks might be solved in due time by their killing all their admirers (XVI).

After listing horrendous examples of mistaken treatment for strangury and illness during pregnancy, he partly blamed the gullible public for the deplorable situation because he thought the quacks had no inducement to improve themselves when "unmeaning impudence, gross imposture, affected importance, and crabbed words will assist them in gaining the character of

skilful Physicians, more than all the advantages of real knowlege" (XIX). Given this situation, he made one of his few non-
satirical suggestions by recommending the state legislature as
the appropriate body to improve medical standards. He rein-
forced his case by citing an earlier attempt at a medical society
to which "the terms of admission were" compared "with those
of the Club of Duellists, mentioned in the Spectator, in which
it was only required of every Candidate to certify that he had
killed his man" (XX). And he included a comparison with the
higher legal admission standards in the sardonic statement that
"The Pettifogger endangers the loss of Estate, the Quack only
of Life," a sentence which recalls the earlier one about "enthusiasts" in "The Meddler."

Much more effective than direct statements were the ap-
proaches in XXXVII and XXXVIII. In the first of the two,
announced as *"Written by the Editor of his works,"* the Correspondent brilliantly employed biblical overtones in the introduction to excoriate the clerical opposition. When the ministers
read, "Then *Philiatros* and L. H. and *Tim Grocer* and the disciples of *Theuth* were assembled; and *Boltrope* also came among
them," they would hear in the background Job 1:6: "Now it
came to pass on the day when the sons of God came to present
themselves before Jehovah, that Satan also came among them."
In the speech which followed, the Correspondent pretended a
conversion but actually condemned the assemblage in acid
irony. In his supposed recantation he said, for example, "I have
believed that an illieterate [*sic*] blunderer, by obtaining a
licence to preach, would not become a proper representative of
the Prophets and Apostles," and "I have believed that religion
would receive little advantage from the virulent controversies
and uncharitable censoriousness of parties." Adding the analogy
from one of Aesop's fables, he compared himself to the dying
lion and Boltrope to the ass; and, in the last portion, he com-
piled a fictitious biography of himself from the contradictory
statements of his antagonists.

The last number of "The Correspondent" consisted of a will,
a fact reflecting the author's legal training. Heavy with satire,
the document specifies which materials are to be left to various
opponents. One provision stated that part of the inheritance
was to be devoted to the Disciples of Theuth after they "incor-

porated by the name of The Society for the Propagation of Riot and Slander, and the Discouragement of Arts and Sciences."

A fact generally unknown is that at one time Trumbull considered reviving "The Correspondent," probably when he had returned from Boston in 1774. In the Cornell Manuscripts there is a first sketch of the resumption and a partial draft of a number. In it, the Correspondent was announced as having "returned again to scourge [the] vices of the times." Part of the article included tales about St. Anthony's shinbone, St. Thomas à Becket, and the Duke of Buckingham. The sketch seemed to promise entertainment, but it probably was best that Trumbull dropped his plan, for he already had enough enemies in New Haven for a beginning lawyer.

"The Correspondent" was a fairly remarkable group of essays for its time, but it is little known today, largely because the then current issues have taken different forms. Trumbull was fortunate in that portion appearing in 1770, for he apparently pleased people who were upset by the squabbles of the metaphysicians. But in 1773 he may have been led to extravagant defensive statement because of the attacks on his writings. As it was, he sometimes displayed a brashness and condescension which angered too many people and lessened his effectiveness. His goal was admirable, but his manner of achieving it was open to objection at times. Had he had more of Addison's approach than Swift's, he might in the long run have convinced more readers. Nonetheless, his achievement was one of which he could be proud. He had proved himself exceptionally able in argumentation, expert in the use of irony, and mature in the handling of prose. And not the least of his virtues was his willingness to challenge eminent persons who objected not to hypocrisy and other vices but to the exposure of them, who wanted the useful appearance of honesty but not the actuality of it. Fortunately, Trumbull had the moral courage and the integrity to withstand both open and indirect threats from those in high places who were powerful but corrupted.

III *"Speculative Essays"*

Another product of the author's busy period from 1769 to 1773 was the unpublished and uncorrected "Speculative Essays."[18]

On the manuscript, Trumbull later wrote, "Begun Anno 1773";
but there are two indications that the compositions should be
dated 1771. First, he made a note that Stephen West's *Essay on
Moral Agency* (1772) came "Within about a Year" after certain
statements in the essays. Second, in a letter to Silas Deane
on January 8, 1772, he mentioned the possibility of a book and
said, "I have sketched out several of these digressory Chapters."
These seem to be the topics with the following titles: "On the
Limits of Human Reason," "On our Idea of Infinity," "Of abstract
Ideas, & general Terms," "On the Foreknowlege & Decrees of
God," "A Critical Dissertation on descriptive Poetry," "On the
Infinite Evil of Sin," and "On the Introduction of Moral Evil."
Of the seven, five were connected with the contemporaneous
religious controversy, the one on abstract ideas dealt only with
philosophy, and that on poetry examined a literary problem.

Though Trumbull was not a deep thinker, he did have the
ability to state lucidly his understanding of abstractions. Noting
the opposition of Pope, Swift, and George Berkeley to John
Locke's conception of "the abstract idea of a man," Trumbull
said "that an abstract idea is so obscure, that it has none of the
marks that distinguish individuals, & yet so plain, that it has all
the marks that denote the species." As an example to illustrate
his contention, he cited the appearance of a man at sunset.
Regrettably, the did not develop his philosophical ideas at
greater length.

He regarded Jonathan Edwards as a great man, but he dis-
liked the disputatiousness of his disciples Samuel Hopkins and
Joseph Bellamy, the latter a person whom he called "one of the
fiercest of these controversial writers."[19] It was against this
background of charges, countercharges, and the like that Trumbull's essays were projected. In the second and sixth essays, he
questioned their use of "infinites," and in the seventh he accused
the metaphysicians of arguing in a circle. Behind his objections
lay not a dislike for theological discussion but a fear that the
heated, as he admitted, disputes would harm Christianity and
benefit the Deists.

But the five essays involved with religious questions are more
significant, for they reveal the attitude of a middle-of-the-road
educated man toward some Calvinistic doctrines and toward the
theological disputes of the era. The thread running through them

is that too great a dependence on reason leads either to scepticism, such as that of Hume, or to the dogmatism of argumentative divines, such as some disciples of Edwards. According to Trumbull, the province of reason is twofold: first, to tell that which is Scripture; and second, "to teach us how to understand what is revealed" in the Bible. As he saw it, the Calvinistic doctrine of predestination was Scriptural, there was a general plan for the universe, and Edwards's supralapsarian position on the entry of sin into the world was right. He also accepted Edwards's distinction between man's natural inability to choose right and his moral inability to do so. Concerning theology Trumbull was more cautious, for he believed that, as soon as man departs from biblical proof and depends on reason, he must hold God responsible for evil.

The "Speculative Essays" are neither polished nor profound, but they have some value for illustrating the interests and observations of Trumbull and for showing some promise of his speculative ability. They are evidence that he was genuinely concerned about theological questions and that his references in other works to metaphysicians stemmed from his strong commitment to his religious beliefs. Undeveloped though these short writings are, they indicated what Trumbull might have done as a serious essayist had he turned in that direction.

In this, his most productive period, Trumbull burst forth with writing which was remarkable both in quantity and quality. "The Meddler," composed of clever imitations and adaptations of the *Tatler* and the *Spectator*, was relatively close to the British periodicals in style and content; but "The Correspondent," which followed immediately, departed from them in spirit and subject matter. His intense purposefulness emphasized instruction and correction rather than amusement, and the topics were ones of immediate concern in the colonial milieu. With three exceptions, all the essays Trumbull contributed to "The Correspondent" were to some degree polemical; a few included light touches, but most were charged with earnestness. Those aimed, perhaps brashly, at the clergy drew the most embittered response in the heated controversy which developed. The unpublished "Speculative Essays" from this period serve mainly to prove their author's genuine interest in both Calvinistic doctrine and in the theological skirmishing of the aftermath of the Great Awakening. Taken as a whole, these writings provided ample proof of their author's knowledge, acuteness, satirical bent, and unwavering principles.

CHAPTER 3

The Progress of Dulness

THE PROGRESS OF DULNESS,[1] second only to *M'Fingal* as Trumbull's best-known work, was a direct, incisive, and sparkling critique of education in its author's time. The three separate parts were advertised in the Connecticut *Journal* as "Part First: Or the Rare Adventures of Tom Brainless"; "Part Second: Or an Essay on the Life and Character of Dick Hairbrain, of finical Memory"; and "Part Third, and Last: Sometimes called, The Progress of Coquetry, or the Adventures of Miss Harriet Simper, of the Colony of Connecticut." Printed in New Haven by Thomas and Samuel Green, the poem was published anonymously. Part I appeared in September 1772, and a second printing of it followed in December of the same year. Part II was released in January 1773; Part III, in September.

The writing and publishing of the last part were contemporaneous with the accelerating battle between Trumbull and his critics in and out of "The Correspondent." The satire was aimed mainly at faults in education, but each section included some strictures about contentious clergy. The Hudibrastic poem was controversial because the author sought to stimulate reform rather than to provide innocuous amusement for his readers. It ridiculed both the mentally slothful, who were too indolent to study, and the metaphysicians, who trusted their reason too far. Apparently with justice, it warned the pastors that they were their own worst enemies. Aimed at encouraging education and morality, it proposed changes which seemed too radical or too offensively stated for some readers. All in all, it was a startling and penetrating evaluation.

Because of the accusations made against Trumbull for some of the ideas in *The Progress of Dulness*, the point needs to be made that he wrote as a friend of religion and education rather than as a foe—indeed, his intense concern for both caused him to ridicule what he considered serious defects in them. As he saw it, both the stupid but orthodox clergymen like Tom Brainless and the intelligent but contentious ones harmed religion by opening the doors for the archenemy—the Deists. And he viewed as weaknesses in education not only the curriculum but also the low standards for college entrance, retention, and graduation. To these corruptions he added the lack of solid academic work for women. His mistake was not in his intention but in the execution of it. Had he initially made his own position clear by granting merits to collegiate education and to the clergy rather than dwelling only on faults, he might have come closer to realizing his objectives and would have saved himself much vituperation.

Trumbull was well qualified for writing a satire on education. Although only twenty-one years of age when he began composing it, he had already developed a vigorous, supple prose style; and, from years of experimentation, he had become proficient in several forms of poetry, especially in the octosyllabic couplet, as the "Epithalamion" attested. And not only did he have command of satire, but he also had the background for understanding and defining the facets of education which he discussed. As the son of a minister and a well-educated minister's wife, as a well-read former student, as a tutor, and as an eligible bachelor, he knew firsthand the material he wove into his poem. And, last, he had the requisite temerity for seeking changes in an educational system which a number of able students found unsatisfactory.

Inasmuch as Trumbull was familiar with British literature, many English poems had influence on *The Progress of Dulness*. Among those suggested by scholars as ones to which he possibly had a literary debt are three which may have contributed hints to the poem as a whole: *Hudibras*, by Butler; "Alma: or, The Progress of the Mind," by Prior; and "The Progress of Poetry," by Swift. Other octosyllabic poems by Goldsmith, Thomas Warton, J. D. Breval, Swift, and Churchill may have suggested ideas which were incorporated into specific parts; and the work of Pope, especially *The Dunciad*, may have affected both subject matter and technique.

But perhaps even more influential than any one of the poems was Swift's "An Apology" preceding *A Tale of a Tub*. As we know from his letter to Silas Deane on January 8, 1772,[2] Trumbull had read "An Apology"; and in it he found the conjunction of religion and education, that he himself made in his letter. Swift had said that "the numerous and gross Corruptions in Religion and Learning might furnish Matter for a Satyr"[3] and that, though religion should not be ridiculed, "surely the Corruptions in it"[4] might be. How much Trumbull was indebted to Swift for these ideas cannot be determined with exactitude, but the fact that the great British satirist mentioned the topics may have precipitated Trumbull's decision to write *The Progress of Dulness*, for the two subjects were already much in his mind and could be united in one poem with a strong emphasis on education.

Several qualities and characteristics of *The Progress of Dulness* should be noted. First, the tone is deliberately varied from section to section. Secondly, the literary allusions refer to works from Greece, Italy, Spain, and England. Third, there is little imagery, and there are few figures of speech. The small number of similes stem from literature and science, a comparison to electricity being the favorite. Fourth, the verse is the jogging tetrameter commonly called Hudibrastic. Whenever there is humor or drollery, the double rhymes, approximate rhymes, and feminine endings occur more frequently. Some examples of humorous rhyming are "laundress"—"salamanders," "fill he"—"Lily," "handsome"—"fancy 'em," "really"—"Pamela," "giddy on"—"meridian," and "rush in"—"blushing." Fifth, the tetrameter couplets often are quotable, as in the following examples: "In all diseases, 'tis expected/ The weakest parts be most infected" and "The man that was not made to think,/ Was born to game, and swear, and drink." And sixth, exposition and description rather than narration are predominant.

The poem seems to have evolved over a period of nearly two years. A preliminary version of Part I probably was composed by late 1771, for early in January 1772 Trumbull wrote to Silas Deane, in reference to the work, that his fear of speaking frankly had caused him to touch lightly on collegiate education and on the clergy. He also expressed a wish not to make more enemies, having only recently become free from his old ones, presumably those irate over the "Epithalamion" and "The Correspondent," numbers I-VIII; and he added that, after considering Deane's suggestions, he might send him a more extended version. Deane's reply to his young friend's letter seems not to be extant, but we do have a later, ebullient message from Trumbull to him, part of which is the following:

As you expect me to repent & amend my ways, you look also I suppose that I should bring forth works meet for repentance—and *that* I shall as fast as possible. This same Progress of Dulness particularly is in the latest Editions become one of the most serious, pious treatises on morals & Divinity, that ever you set eyes on. I wrote it at first in a pretty free stile, said humorous things where I could & severe ones where I pleased; but I have so many serious folks at my elbows, that they have made me alter almost half of it, throw out every stroke of humour, that in the least exaggerated the descriptions beyond truth, & lay aside every satirical reflection that had any thing of my airs of impudence & defiance in it. So that on the whole if it should be published, it will be thought as well-meaning & harmless a piece, as a halfway-cov'nant Dialogue.[5]

Trumbull concluded with a promise that he would bring a copy to Wethersfield in May so that Deane might examine it. This letter and the one in January offer proof that Deane acted as a literary advisor to the Yale tutor by suggesting topics, methods of treatment, and a place of publication. The March letter necessitates a re-evaluation of Trumbull's boldness and courage in writing the poem. One scholar has spoken of the author's "temperamental caution";[6] and another has written, "His friends, as usual, encouraged him to be valiant rather than discreet...."[7] Trumbull's own words testify that it was he who was audacious and his friends who were prudent.

I   *"Within Yourselves Your Danger Lies"*

In the preface to the first part,[8] Trumbull says that his "subject is the state of the times in regard to literature and religion" and that he plans to cite "those general errors, that hinder the advantages of education and the growth of piety." Using Tom's career to illustrate his views, he asserts "that to the frequent scandal, as well of religion, as learning, a fellow, without any share of genius, or application to study, may pass with credit through life, receive the honours of a liberal education, and be admitted to the right hand of fellowship among ministers of the gospel;—that except in one neighboring province, ignorance wanders unmolested at our colleges, examinations are dwindled to mere form and ceremony, and after four years dozing there, no one is ever refused the honors of a degree, on account of dulness and insufficiency." In gracefully controlled prose, the author states his other convictions: that knowledge of ancient languages, mathematics, and metaphysics is of small practical application; that study of English grammar, composition, and style would be worthwhile; that numerous incompetent men become ministers; and that contemporary religious quarrels "have done more hurt to the cause of religion, than all the malice, the ridicule, and the folly of its enemies."

Tom Brainless, the strong young man serving as the main vehicle for satire in Part I, incarnates an incorrigible laziness which would defeat all attempts at education, good or bad. In preparation for college, he is sent to study with a clergyman, who unfortunately has lost his knowledge of languages, with the result that the combination of teacher's incompetence and learner's laziness produces minimal progress in Latin and Greek. After two years of such educational stumbling, Tom goes to college, accompanied and recommended by his parson and his father. There he goes to classes unprepared, pleads a variety of illnesses, and dozes his way through four years unmolested and uneducated. For knowledge of languages he, as well as others like him, is aptly described in the couplet, "And for our linguists, fairly try them,/ A tutor'd parrot might defy them." But he is graduated because no one fails the final examination.

After graduation, Tom is thrown on his own by his father, who advises him to teach and then become a minister. Tom follows his advice, first becoming a schoolmaster, then studying with a clergyman for six months, during which time he learns hair-splitting techniques and labyrinthine theological nuances. When he goes before an assemblage of clergymen to prove his fitness, he is not held to demonstrating either learning or sense, for they are not the desiderata: "What though his skull is cudgel-proof!/ He's orthodox, and that's enough." Receiving approval from the assembled ministers, Tom is licensed to preach and goes to a sleepy parish where he "Does little good, and little harm."

Trumbull contends that not only the slothful students such as Tom but all the others are hampered by an inadequate curriculum, one in which, as he later wrote, "English poetry and the belles-lettres were called folly, nonsense and an idle waste of time."[9] According to him, the fact that the instructors teach only the dead languages results in the students' losing the rhetorical graces of English while becoming incompetent scholars of Greek and Latin. Their ludicrous approximations in a Classical language is vividly pictured in the following lines:

> Think how would Tully stare or smile
> At these wan spectres of his style,
> Or Horace in his jovial way
> Ask what these babblers mean to say. (19)

Furthermore, Trumbull argues, the students are subjected to excessive reliance on syllogistic reasoning, memorization of Greek names for figures of speech, and overemphasis on mathematics; and they are encouraged in vain metaphysical speculations. The curriculum against which he protests probably was much like that scheduled by President Stiles for 1779.[10]

The revised curriculum which Trumbull wants is one which, as Howard has mentioned,[11] embodies precepts of Lord Kames and others of the Scottish common-sense school:

> Our youths might learn each nobler art,
> That shews a passage to the heart;
> From ancient languages well known
> Transfuse new beauties to our own;
> With taste and fancy well refin'd,
> Where moral rapture warms the mind,
> From schools dismiss'd, with lib'ral hand,
> Spread useful learning o'er the land;
> And bid the eastern world admire
> Our rising worth, and bright'ning fire. (23)

These ideas stressing a combination of the practical and the fine arts taught with sound judgment are the ones for which not only Trumbull but also Joseph Howe and Timothy Dwight were campaigning. They had some small success in establishing a taste for rhetoric and declamation, with the result, as Dwight later expressed it, that "The period from 1771 to 1777 will ever be considered as forming an era in the history of the College."[12]

In connection with Trumbull's point about metaphysical speculations he reiterates views stated in the "Speculative Essays" and in "The Correspondent":

> Indulgent heaven to man below,
> Hath all explain'd we need to know;
> Hath clearly taught enough to prove
> Content below, and bliss above. (22)

Such ideas put Trumbull at odds with a whole group of divines and especially with the two men whose names were represented by asterisks in the couplet "Armies of pens draw forth to fight,/ And x x x x and x x x x write." The names of the two leading metaphysical controversialists, Bellamy and Hopkins, fit the meter neatly. In challenging such prominent men among the clergy, the young tutor displayed genuine courage.

This brashness is strong medicine, of course, but some of his statements are even stronger. It is true that Trumbull allies himself with the clergy in condemning scoffers against religion and that he insists upon his amicable intentions:

> Ye fathers of our church attend
> The serious counsels of a friend,
> Whose utmost wish, in nobler ways,
> Your sacred dignity to raise.
> Though blunt the style, the truths set down
> Ye can't deny—though some may frown. (29)

But, when he insists upon the accuracy of his charges, some ministers would find especially galling the accusation that just as thieves once sought sanctuary in a church, dull students often find refuge by joining the clerical ranks. And, if this were not enough, Trumbull exhorts the men accustomed to doing the exhorting when he warns that the enemy from within is more dangerous than the one from without: "The deist's scoffs you may despise;/ Withing yourselves your danger lies." It may well be that this admonition provoked some of the bitterest reaction to the poem.

Part I is the most vigorous, ebullient, and substantial of the three sections. It contains an abundance of double rhymes, feminine endings, and literary allusions, among which are those to Classical mythology, Homer, Roman legend, Livy, Virgil, Cicero, Horace, Vida, Milton, Abraham Cowley, and George Buchanan. Trumbull may have obtained some ideas from the tetrameter poems listed earlier and from Thomas Warton's *The Progress of Discontent*. Replete with satirical shafts aimed at lazy students, low entrance and graduation standards, a questionable curriculum, semi-educated ministers, and controversial metaphysicians, *The Progress of Dulness*, Part I, was designed less to entertain than to correct. Its reform function might have been more successful, however, had the author sought improvement not by shaming but by persuading.

II *"The Clockwork Gentleman Is Made"*

When the reaction to Part I was powerful and bitter, Trumbull prefaced Part II with a stinging message *"To the Envious and Malicious Reader,"*[13] in the manner of Swift's reference to "the ill-placed Cavils of the Sour, the Envious, the Stupid, and Tastless"[14] in "An Apology." Enumerating some of the charges made against him, Trumbull said he had been accused of writing verse which was "both scurrilous in the sentiments and dirty in the style," of being "either a Separatist, or a Sandemanian" and of being "an open reviler of the Clergy, and an enemy to truth and learning." Irritated by these charges, he defended himself and challenged replies, especially from "the haughtiest Dullard, and the most impertinent Coxcomb of this age"; but, in general, he relied less on personal attack and more on the tactically superior invitation to his accusers to check the accuracy of the picture before belaboring the artist. In the long run, however, he regretted the barbed preface and did not have it printed again.

As Trumbull pictures it, the career of Dick Hairbrain in Part II consists of another travesty on education. Even on his way to college, Dick, who contrasts with Tom by being the son of a wealthy farmer, meditates cynically on his future school life, thinking of carefree, riotous living in a place where money will pay for infractions of rules and laws. At college, he appears as an awkward "Country Fop" at first, but he gradually becomes a polished one. He avoids serious study but excels in some non-academic skills such as gambling, cards, and turbulent nocturnal revels; and he follows the path of the typical fop of the times, in which ostentation, impertinence, and obscenity were regarded with more favor than genuine merit. As a result, dandies wear expensive ruffles, brooches, coats, hats, and stockings. With the aid of a barber and a dancing master, the fop is further improved; but he needs polished manners and light reading. From France, he obtains meretricious compliments and shallow jests that impress young coquettes. To store his brain, he can

> From endless loads of novels gain
> Soft, simp'ring tales of amorous pain,
> With double meanings, neat and handy,
> From Rochester and Tristram Shandy. (44)

Dick's postcollege career is a sad one. Having avoided serious study himself, he encourages others to "scoff at college educations." He travels to Europe, adds to his foppishness and refines it, pays court to numerous ladies, and serves as a model for other less skilled fops. But he runs into debt, loses his health, and sinks into lonely declining years.

Part II differs markedly from its predecessor. Because of the deliberate change in tone which Trumbull explained in the preface to this section, there is less jocularity and drollery. And, because the author already had attacked so many academic ills in the first part, he was able to limit his ridicule to one target in the second and give it more unity. His target also seems less objectionable because a fop was a commonly accepted butt of ridicule. The literary allusions are not so wide-ranging as those in Part I: of the ancients, Cicero is mentioned; and of the British, Pope, Watts, Laurence Sterne, and Lord Rochester. Of possible literary antecedents, additional ones are J. D. Breval's *The Progress of a Rake*; Churchill's *The Ghost*, in which Book IV opens with coxcombs and fops; and Churchill's *The Duellist*, in which Book III includes a lord who lived riotously, somewhat like Dick. Though the subject matter was appropriate for light treatment, it received sober scorn and condemnation.

Countering the malicious accusations of his opponents, whom

he charged with deliberately misunderstanding his intentions, Trumbull reviled scoffers who derided their alma mater: "Whoe'er at college points his sneer,/ Proves that himself learn'd nothing there." There is only one explicit shaft of ridicule directed at religious faults or foibles. When, after reading Hume, Voltaire, and Henry Bolingbroke, Dick rails against revealed religion, Trumbull blames not only the fop but also the clergy:

> For where's the theme that beaux could hit
> With least similitude of wit,
> Did not religion and the priest
> Supply materials for the jest? (48)

And, over all, the object of the satire is the main character Dick rather than the college or the clergy, though both student and school are held up to scorn in the description of his graduation as *"Pro meritis."*

III *"The Fair Are Nursed in Folly's School"*

Introducing the third part, Trumbull announced his theme as follows: "My design in this poem is to show, that the foibles we discover in the fair sex arise principally from the neglect of their education, and the mistaken notions they imbibe in their early youth." Through the career of Harriet Simper, these ideas are illustrated. Even when she is young, she is advised to look pretty and be bold. A little later, she is sent to a city for education in the social graces and in fashion; she learns much about them, returns quite vain, and reads only sentimental novels. Now she practices what she has been educated for—being a coquette. Rejecting all suitors, she flirts with many; but, when Dick Hairbrain returns from Europe, she succumbs to his charms. He does not respond, however, and Harriet is gradually supplanted as a coquette by younger girls who have had the misfortune to receive the same education as she. When Parson Tom comes courting, accompanied by a deacon just as Don Quixote was by Sancho Panza, she marries him; and they settle down to a dull life in a rural parish.

An education such as Harriet's is presented as both demeaning and deleterious. Able to learn solid and useful material, Har-

riet and her cohorts are restricted to the merely social, one result
of which is baneful gossiping. In some of the more slashing
lines, Harriet and other belles are seen at tea talking fashion
and verbally pillorying absent girls:

> "And were you at the ball last night?
> Well, Chloe look'd like any fright;
> Her day is over for a toast;
> She'd now do best to act a ghost." (73)

Then Fanny and Coelia are given like uncharitable treatment.
It is for such silly but injurious activities that Harriet's education has prepared her—not for usefulness and happiness.

In Trumbull's view, the reading the young ladies do is
particularly harmful because it distorts their sense of values:

> For 'tis esteem, coquettes dispense
> Tow'rd learning, genius, worth and sense,
> Sincere affection, truth refined,
> And all the merit of the mind.
> But love's the passion they experience
> For gold, and dress, and gay appearance.
> For ah! what magic charms and graces
> Are found in golden suits of laces! (83)

The author maintains that when a lady's reading is limited to
novels and plays, she imagines herself as a young Pamela and
hopes for a Grandison or a Lovelace. Harriet, under the influence of such reading, rejects suitors, including the worthy ones
whom she says she "esteems."

Just as in the second part he had made only one reference
to ministerial opposition, so in the last part he inserted a single
barb. Drawing a parallel from the way some belles see evil in
small actions of a rival, Trumbull thrusts at his critics:

> So priests drive poets to the lurch
> By fulminations of the church,
> Mark in our title-page our crimes,
> Find heresies in double rhymes,
> Charge tropes with damnable opinion,
> And prove a metaphor, Arminian,

> Peep for our doctrines, as at windows,
> And pick out creeds of inuendoes [*sic*]. (75)

In his neat, precise way, he taunted his opponents with the two couplets of double rhymes, as if defying them to read any heresy into them.

Part III is quite different from either of the preceding ones. It reveals less strong feeling than the others, possibly because it was supporting improved female education rather than opposing specific abuses. In tone, it reverts to Part I's jocularity because the author had found that the readers preferred it to the more elevated style of Part II. Among the small number of literary allusions, the most obvious are to Samuel Richardson, John Bunyan, and Cervantes. In subject matter, this last section is more radical than the others because advocating improved education for girls was not common at the time. As early as 1770, he had urged better education for the ladies when he had delivered his master's oration, from which he quoted at the end of the preface. For literary antecedents, it has been suggested that he may have been familiar with Goldsmith's "The Double Transformation" or with Swift's "Phillis, Or, the Progress of Love," "The Furniture of a Woman's Mind," and "Cadenus and Vanessa." In the last of these, the gossiping ladies are a parallel and possibly a source.

It usually has been thought that Trumbull was relying almost exclusively on his reading of English literature in Part III, but two items in the Burton Manuscripts which have particular bearing on "The Progress of Coquetry" indicate otherwise. Quoting from Watts's *Psalms*, he headed a draft of an essay with a two-line epigraph, "I've seen an end of what we call/ Perfection here below," lines close to those in Part II, "And in their wisest progress show/ Perfection is not found below." Part of the manuscript reads:

In the early part of my life, I was very intimately acquainted with a young Lady of great Beauty & Vivacity, but very romantic in her temper, & one who had formed her Ideas of life not from experience, but from the flights of her own imagination & the exaggerated & unnatural descriptions, which abound in Novels & Romances. She held a regular Correspondence with two other Ladies of very similar Characters & dispositions. By my intimacy with her I procured a

sight of several of their Letters. The Subject was Matrimony. Her
principal Correspondent had introduced it by a panegyric on the
happiness of a single life, & a list of the extraordinary qualifications
the Gentleman must possess who could persuade her to change her
situation & part with her liberty.

The aspiring ladies assured each other that they would be
satisfied with nothing less than perfection in a husband; but
one married a rich coxcomb, another stole out of town to marry
a man politically unpopular, and the third was unmarried,
though she had had romances with unworthy and unsavory men.
Immediately following the essay is the unpublished "Epitaph
to be inscribed on the Marriage Bed of Miss S ... W ...," dated
1773. The young lady enjoyed the role of *"Toast* & Coquette" for
several years and rejected all suitors. With the passage of time,
though, she changed her mind:

> ... her Character becoming known,
> And the list of her Lovers not increasing,
> As She verged toward years of Discretion,
> Which in Coquettes commence at Twenty-four,
> She shuddered at the Prospect
> of the dreary Vale of Virginity,
> And trembled at the dreadful Tales
> Of Old Maids leading Apes in Hell:
> Which as She now dreaded as her Lot,
> She resolved either as by way of Prevention,
> Or preparatory Work,
> To associate herself with One in this World.
>
> On the . . . day of . . . Ad 1772,
> She married J . . . S . . . .

The groom, according to Trumbull, was as worthless as the
fellow Captain Kidd had reputedly buried on top of his
treasure.

Although Trumbull did not indicate any connection between
the two drafts and *The Progress of Dulness,* they obviously have
relevance to the question of derivativeness. J. S. may have furnished details for the portrait of Dick Hairbrain, and Miss S. W.
may have provided much of Harriet Simper. Second in his class
according to economic ranking, Trumbull knew a number of

Connecticut coquettes, as he clearly implies in a letter of September 10, 1773, to Miss Sally Lloyd of Stamford. Perhaps one of these ladies wrote on the title page of a copy of Part II now in the Beinecke Library of the Yale University Library, "By John Tru[m]bull as f[ini]cal as Di[ck]." Be that as it may, the assertion that Harriet seems "suspiciously similar to coquettes in contemporary and earlier British literature"[15] needs qualification. While the well-read author knew examples in English books, he indubitably was aware of living models in his own colony.

Not only is there proof that he knew colonial coquettes, but there is clear evidence that he was acquainted with a group of bright girls who had excellent educational potential. This fact is obvious from several delightfully witty and mildly flirtatious paragraphs in his letter to Miss Lloyd. The tone of the missive is well represented by the following sentence, in which he mentions his poem:

Not studious of revenge, we shall leave you all to the stings of your own consciences; desiring you only in your calm hours of contemplation, to consider seriously what right any or all of you had to rise so much above the common level of your Sex, which, in this colony, I will venture to say, is not unjustly described in the Progress of Coquetry (just published) which I desire you all (as others do) to read at your leisure, censure the Writer & apply to your neighbors—

His contention was that young ladies like Miss Sally Lloyd and her friends, as well as others less clever, deserved a more solid preparation for life.

In the first months of 1773 material related to *The Progress of Dulness* intentionally or otherwise appeared in the Connecticut *Journal.* The amount was small when we consider the polemic nature of the poem, which contained something of what Trumbull referred to as his "airs of impudence & defiance." On January 8, a twenty-six line poem on a fop was printed, and immediately below it was "An Observation on Debauchery and Foppery." The timing was fortunate, because Part II on Dick Hairbrain was about to be published, and the second piece specifically said about foppery, "Here then, is a subject for our wit and railla[r]y; here let us point our satire." Two weeks later came a reply in thirty lines of Hudibrastic verse accusing the author of the "Observation" of being a fop himself. The most extended notice was the series of questions posed by a "Querist" on January 29 in a letter addressed "To the Author of the Progress of Dulness, Parts first, and second":

Question 1. Had you any other design at bottom than to show your wit, and see how much diversion you could make at the expence of others? and do you think the subjects you chose, proper to be treated with ridicule?
2. Why do you rail so much against Metaphysics? Let us how [*sic*], if you please, how far you imagine reason may be used in our enquiries about Religion, and whether at all, or not?
3. Will you not allow there is a great share of self-confidence and assurance, shewn in the Preface to your second part? And do not you mean to insinuate in your Dedication to the Envious and Malicious Reader, that all who have not the wisdom to think just as you do, have found fault with your Poems out of nothing but mere envy and malice?
4. Why did you choose out a poor man's sons for the subject of your satire? and tell us that your Tom's father's incomes were but small, and Dick's was but a farmer?
5. Do you think it is just to cast personal reflections? Who are the Persons marked out by stars? Who is the haughtiest Dullard and most impertinent Coxcomb of the age? and who are the Rev'd Gentlemen, that have signalized themselves by calling their enemies, Heretics, Deists, and Arminians?

This letter provoked a clever response addressed *"To my good Catechist"* by Trumbull, who answered the questions in the issue of February 5, 1773. Ably and clearly, he demonstrated that he was not merely being witty, that he supported religion, that a dull character is ridiculous, and that some of the questions merited "no serious notice." And he stated once again his position on the place of reason in religion:

Reason was given to assist us, in explaining the word of God, not in going beyond it—in determining what are the essential doctrines of Christianity, not in prying into mysteries, which the Divine Being hath never designed to unfold—in understanding and enforcing the precepts of Religion, which are delivered with such plainness and perspicuity, that the wayfaring man, *though a fool, need not err therein*; not in turning Theology into such an intricate Science, that not one in twenty of the deepest students can comprehend it, nor in raising vain systems of mystical philosophy, the air-built castles of a speculative brain, nor under pretence of discovering new doctrines in the Gospel, adding to divine Revelation, a vain-glorious supplement of metaphysical disquisitions.

As a clever polemicist, Trumbull also pointed out the inconsistency in his querist's asking the identity of the dullard and the coxcomb after the protest about casting "personal reflections."

After Trumbull's response to the published questions, three bits of verse were printed which may have been related to *The Progress of Dulness*. First, on February 26 a twenty-seven-line tetrameter poem called "The Rake" described a dissolute character whose career in vice had affinities with that of Dick Hairbrain. Then on March 5 came the cleverest reaction to Trumbull's satire in the form of thirty-six lines of pentameter. After referring to *Don Quixote*, just as Trumbull later does in Part III, the versifier described "Prose" going on a walk and meeting "Pony," obviously the short Trumbull. When Prose mounts Pony to ride away, the poetaster called the combination "Bombast." No other attacks were printed, possibly because attention was focused on "The Correspondent," recently revived; but there was one more related item. Thirty lines of tetrameter describing gossiping ladies were printed on April 23, a far less clever description than Trumbull's, which appeared in Part III a few months later.

In his reply to the "querist," Trumbull also mentioned support for his poem. Friends in New Haven and Silas Deane in Wethersfield must have encouraged him, and Joseph Howe wrote from Killingly on February 26. The relevant portion of Howe's letter is as follows:

But what I mean to rally you for, is for being a good Poet, a great Wit & a Satirist.—Nay, do not flinch. The Story is got all over Boston. The other day a Gentleman came to me and said, *I am told you are acquainted with Mr. Trumbull, the Author of the Progress of Dulness.* Sir, Said I, stroking my Face down with an Air of Satisfaction, I have the Honour to be particularly acquainted with him. *Pray of what Age is he?*—About 24. *Twenty four?* replied he with some Surprize,

I should have Thought he had been Sixty. His Prose is equal to Swift's, & his Poetry to Butler's. I had not the Temerity to Contradict him, nor indeed an Inclination for it. If I had, I suppose it would not have been of any Avail. For he was none of your Second Edition people. But, undoubtedly, the first *Classical* Scholar in Boston. Mr. James Lovel [*sic*], whom possibly you may have heard of.[16]

Despite the raillery by Howe and the obviously inflated estimate of the prose and the verse, Trumbull could take comfort in the fact that the competent scholar Lovell thought highly of his work.

In any case, *The Progress of Dulness* attracted the attention of many educated colonials and drew a mixed response. Those agreeing with the author or appreciating the literary merits of the poem were free with their plaudits, and those smarting from the satirical whip belabored him lustily. The opposition, it may be noted, assailed the writer rather than the uncomfortable truths told in vigorous couplets.

Critics usually have rated the poem a clever success. In 1829, Samuel Kettell wrote of its "felicitous power of sarcasm"[17] and thought it should rank as high as *M'Fingal,* and Samuel Knapp thought the satire had been effective.[18] The *American Annual Register for the Year 1831-32* called the poem "successful as a satire."[19] In 1856, A. P. Peabody, writing in the *North American Review,* called it "sprightly and harmonious";[20] and in the year preceding, Duyckincks' *Cyclopaedia of American Literature* said it might still be read with pleasure;[21] but in 1865 Frederick Sheldon wrote that "all that have survived" are two lines about the Reverend Brainless: "On Sunday in his best array/ Deals forth the dulness of the day."[22] However, some recent critics have praised it. Howard calls it "a poem that was as individual as any other of its kind,"[23] and Cowie speaks of "the high degree of poetical merit which it possesses."[24]

Something of a literary event in its time, the poem became a historical piece in a few years because the swift-moving events of the Revolutionary War period and subsequent years focused interest on nationalism and attendant problems. Part I was reprinted in 1787-88 in the *American Magazine,* of which Noah Webster was the editor; but the work as a whole seems not to have been reprinted until 1794 (Exeter). It was quickly followed by editions in 1797 (Carlisle) and 1801 (Wrentham).

Later it was included in Trumbull's *Poetical Works* (1820), in the *Colonnade*, Volume XIV (1922), and in Vernon Louis Parrington's *The Connecticut Wits* (1926). More recently it has been reprinted in *The Satiric Poems of John Trumbull: The Progress of Dulness and M'Fingal*, edited by Edwin T. Bowden (1962), and in the facsimile editions of the *Poetical Works*. It has, of course, been anthologized frequently.

The Progress of Dulness is an astringent, accurate, and timely satire about education written by a fearless, brash, and honest man. It reveals its author's intense zeal for reform by its clear and concise portrait of contemporary ills in collegiate education and by its support for a more academic training for women. It maintains effective and readable thrusts at outmoded concepts by a writer who was at ease with his medium. Though its many brilliant parts do not add up to a smooth artistic whole, it still attracts us with the clever satirical lines about the prevailing educational system which yielded sad results for nearly every Tom, Dick, and Harriet.

CHAPTER 4

M'Fingal

M'FINGAL,[1] the principal work for which we know Trumbull, has had a distinctive role in American culture and history. It had its origin in some of its author's patriotic verse and in the urging of some members of the Continental Congress who perceived the necessity to raise colonial morale by ridiculing the British. The first canto was written and printed in the last months of 1775 and was published early in 1776. In 1782, the author expanded the poem to four cantos by dividing the first one of 1776 into two with some modifications and by adding a third and fourth.

The first two cantos of the completed satire dealt with a town meeting in which M'Fingal and Honorius debate contemporary issues, the former supporting the Tory side and the latter the Whig. The third involved a liberty pole, a mock-heroic individual combat, and a tarring and feathering. The fourth presented a vision of the events of the Revolutionary War, including the surrender of Cornwallis. Intended as mock epic, it was written in Hudibrastic verse which moved more like that of Swift and Churchill than that by Butler. It satirized the opponents of the colonial Whigs mainly through a Scotch Tory who derived his name from James Macpherson's Ossianic *Fingal: An Ancient Epic Poem* (1762). Trumbull's *M'Fingal* contained many allusions not only to the epics by Homer, Virgil, and Milton but also to the Bible. *M'Fingal* had an impact during the war which is difficult to assess but which was probably strongest on the educated classes because of its literary nature. The fact that the completed poem was pirated in 1782 helped bring about copyright laws in Connecticut, but editions were printed in other places without the knowledge or consent of the author. The poem made him famous, and, ironically, gave him the name M'Fingal in the popular mind. Begun in a dark hour in American history, *M'Fingal* became associated with patriotism in times of crisis; and it has entered into our national heritage as an important legacy.

I *Background*

Behind *M'Fingal* lay Trumbull's consistent record of support for liberty. He probably was encouraged in his love of freedom by his home environment at Watertown, for at one time he referred to his father as "the highest whig"[2] in town. At Yale, as part of the resistance to what the colonists considered encroachments on rights and privileges, he vigorously spoke out in his master's oration in 1770[3] to praise "heroic love of Liberty," "manly fortitude," and "generosity of sentiment" as pledges of coming glory. Moreover, he took an unequivocal stand with the Whigs in the following statement: "And I cannot but hope, notwithstanding some dangerous examples of infamous defection, that there is a spirit remaining in these Colonies, that will invariably oppose itself to the efforts of usurpation and perfidy, and forbid that Avarice should ever betray us to Slavery." Though he rarely mentioned in "The Correspondent" the political struggle over liberty, that he was aware of it is apparent from two of the essays. On February 12, 1773, he made a passing reference to "the ferment of politics" as "being pretty much subsided";[4] and a few weeks later he devoted an entire essay to "Public Spirit,"[5] a virtue which he thought too short-lived.

After Trumbull left New Haven for Boston in the fall of 1773, he continued his patriotic work while he read law with John Adams and lived in the home of Thomas Cushing, Speaker of the House of Representatives. Trumbull seems to have established himself early as a keen and reliable young man. In the Adams household he was regarded as a "genius"[6] and was enough of a confidant to be trusted in discussions of critical issues such as reactions to the Boston Tea Party.[7] Furthermore, he was esteemed also by an association of patriots of which "John Adams, John Hancock, Samuel Adams and Elbridge Gerry, were prominent members."[8] This band of patriots clearly saw

the nature of the task ahead and advocated the requisite political measures. According to Trumbull, "To cement the union of
all the colonies, to counteract the fears of the people and encourage their confidence in their own strength and resources,
to lead them into measures decisive in their consequences, and
to prepare their minds for resistance by arms, was the only
policy which the leaders could, at that time, pursue."[9]

To advocate that policy, the group met and decided about
what political topics essays should be written, who should do
the writing, and to which newspapers the articles should be
sent. For the meetings, Trumbull served for some time as "a
confidential secretary,"[10] and he often contributed political
articles for publication.[11] Specific essays have not yet been
attributed to him, probably because their identification has
been made difficult by his careful efforts to keep them
anonymous.[12]

In the very eye of the political storm beginning to rage,
Trumbull was a witness and a participant in the exciting historical period which, as he later suggested to C. A. Goodrich,
could best be depicted with the aid of surviving persons who
had participated in the events or saw them.[13] The Boston Tea
Party was staged when he was there, and it may be that he
not only was in the crowd surrounding the "Indians" but had
an even closer link with the affair.[14] And the Tea Party led to
the Boston Port Bill, which provoked a united colonial opposition
to Great Britain. In Trumbull's anonymous political articles
he may have attacked the bill, as did the able young lawyer
Josiah Quincy, whose Observations on ... the Boston Port Bill
was published in May, 1774; but, if Trumbull did so, his contribution is not yet identified. In August of the same year, however, he made a verse attack on the bill in his first-known patriotic poem, "An Elegy on the Times," which was published
anonymously in two installments in the Massachusetts Spy on
September 22 and 29, 1774,[15] and later included in his Poetical
Works.

II   Other Patriotic Poems

"An Elegy on the Times" may seem stuffy to twentieth-century
readers, but the style was popular in the eighteenth century.

In the verse form of Gray's "Elegy Written in a Country Church-yard," it consists of sixty-eight stanzas decrying contemporary British policies, forecasting the greatness of America, and predicting a decline in fortunes for Britain. The poem begins with a picture of past glory:

> Oh Boston! late with every beauty crown'd,
> Where Commerce triumph'd on the fav'ring gales;
> And each pleased eye, that roved in prospect round,
> Hail'd thy bright spires and bless'd thy opening sails!

Another stanza says the colonists have unsuccessfully presented their case to the mother country. Despite contemporary harassment and provocation, the poet advises restraint: "Nor basely blend, too daring but in vain,/ Th' assassin's madness with the patriot's zeal." For the future, the poet predicts great American cities and armies stationed "Where cold Ontario's icy waves are roll'd,/ Or far Altama's silver waters glide!" Contrasting with the happy American future is an ignominious one for Britain:

> From those loved seats, the Virtues sad withdrew
> From fell Corruption's bold and venal hand;
> Reluctant Freedom waved her last adieu,
> And devastation swept the vassall'd land.

> On her white cliffs, the pillars once of fame,
> Her melancholy Genius sits to wail,
> Drops the fond tear, and o'er her latest shame,
> Bids dark Oblivion draw th' eternal veil.

Trumbull presumably thought a serious style more suitable and effective; and in this judgment he could have been right for his time because his New Haven friends praised the elegy as his best work.[16] Modern readers, however, give the poem a different evaluation. Repelled by the personifications, elisions, and relentless modification of nouns, they think the piece one of his less successful efforts. It should be noted, though, that Cowie has said that "in writing 'An Elegy on the Times,' Trumbull was acting for the first time (albeit anonymously) as a spokesman for the entire country,"[17] and that lack of fieriness probably has been misunderstood. The poem has been called "very mild indeed"[18] and estimated as "a reasoned message of prudence arising out of Trumbull's innate conservatism";[19] but, in the light of the times when it was written, it appears less innocuous. Given the tense contemporary situation, Trumbull was tactically right in urging restraint rather than armed conflict, for advocacy of the latter would have been premature and treasonable.

Except for *M'Fingal*, Trumbull's only other known patriotic verse during the Revolution was "The Genius of America; An Ode," a thirteen-stanza poem which he composed in 1777 after the Battle of Saratoga and which he lengthened by the addition of three stanzas after the Battle of Monmouth in 1778. This long patriotic poem unfortunately has the same faults as "An Elegy on the Times" without having many of its virtues.

Far more important than the "Elegy" for the development of *M'Fingal* is "By Thomas Gage ... A Proclamation," which evolved over a period of three months in the spring and summer of 1775. Shortly after publishing the elegy, Trumbull returned to New Haven, began practicing law, and was getting established in his profession when in May 1775 Silas Deane apparently wrote him a letter requesting a burlesque version of General Gage's battlefield encounters. On May 27, Trumbull replied,[20] saying first that for over a year he had written no verse except the elegy. Then he raised questions about the requested poem:

A humorous Essay, or piece of burlesque, you will perhaps tell me would strike the public Attention, tho' a Serious performance might be disregarded—As far as I have observed nobody feels much disposed to humour on this Subject, or thinks the State of the Times any laughing matter.—But suppose such a piece to succeed—What would be its Effect?—It would inspire us with Contempt of the British Troops, of their Courage, their strength & the skill & understanding of their Leaders—Should we fight the better for that temper—The Army, who despise their Enemies, are most easily thrown into a Pannic [*sic*] & discompiled—The Soldier will be most couragious [*sic*], who expects danger, but defies it, & who is animated not by a spirit of ridicule & the affected jingle of Hudibrastic rhymes, but a zeal & ardour that borders on desperation—It would throw Contempt on the Tories—But can they be viewed by the Continent as greater Objects of Detestation, than they are already considered—They cannot—I have other grounds of Diffidence—Had I (which I have not at present) the same Flow of Vivacity & Spirits, which assisted me formerly in the production of those essays, which perhaps have given you too favorable an Opinion of my Abilities, I should doubt much of the Success of this project. The whole subject is so merely a *Nothing,* that it must be a kind of Creation to make any thing of it—Yet to give a Narration of Facts, leaves no room for Invention—I mean for Fiction, which is of as much Advantage to a humorous as to a Serious Poem—Witness Hudibras, the Rape of the Lock, the Dunciad, The Dispensary, the Lutrin—all, Poems of unequalled Humour, which owe half their beauties to the graces of Fiction—Besides, would not the high Burlesque, the style of the Dunciad, for instance—suit this subject better than the low style of Hudibras, & be easier adapted to a serious turn in a subsequent Canto, according to your plan of varying the Style in different parts—A pompous parade & nothing done—Loud menaces & nobody hurt—Much thunder & no houses struck—This has been the Style of Gage's Campaigning & would call, I think for a similar style of [Narration]. You desired me to think on the Subject & w[rite] you. I have done so—I have writ all I have thought on it—I will not absolutely determine, till I hear from you again.—Perhaps I may by & by send you a small Poem on the late Battle in the Massachusetts, which I had just begun, when I rec^d your letter. You shall have it, if ever it is finished.

I am Sir with much Esteem
Your obliged Friend &
humble Servant
John Trumbull

P. S. My respects to
Mr J. Adams
Friends here are all well

This letter contains several points significant for understanding the genesis and development of the poem. First, the young lawyer already had been composing a poem on "the late Battle in the Massachusetts," presumably Lexington and Concord. Next, it may be deduced that Deane had suggested a Hudibrastic or low burlesque "Narration of Facts" concerning Gage's modest military triumphs with several parts in varying styles. And last, Deane and others perceived much more clearly than Trumbull the necessity of ridiculing the British and Tories.

Because we do not have the complete correspondence, not all of the next steps leading toward the composition of *M'Fingal* in the fall can be established definitively; a number of them, however, can be ascertained. The sequence of events and actions which may be relevant began on June 12, 1775, when Gage issued another of his proclamations. On June 18 in Philadelphia, where Silas Deane was attending the Continental Congress, he made an entry in his diary that he had written to Mr. Trumbull (probably John Trumbull the poet). On June 19, the Connecticut *Courant* in Hartford published the proclamation. On July 15, Deane again noted in his diary a letter to "Trumbull." On July 17, Philip Freneau's burlesque of the proclamation appeared in the Connecticut *Courant*. Then on August 7 and 14 Trumbull's burlesque of the proclamation was published by the same paper—anonymously, of course. Usually shortened to "By Thomas Gage ... A Proclamation," the full title is as follows:

> By Thomas Gage, whom British Frenzy
> Stiled Honourable and Excellency,
> O'er Massachusetts sent to stand here
> Vice-Admiral and Chief Commander,
> Whose Power Gubernatorial still
> Extends as far as Bunker-Hill,
> Whose Admiralty reaches clever
> Full half a mile up Mystic River;
> Let ev'ry Clime and ev'ry Nation
> Attend once more,
> A Proclamation.

In a parody full of bombast, irony, and Hudibrastic rhymes, Trumbull ridiculed Gage's style and ideas. He had the proclamation declaring, for example, that "The good effects we saw in visions,/ Of lordships, pensions, posts, commissions" have been lost. Continuing, Gage said the colonists "Denied the sacred rights to these/ Of calmly robbing whom they please"; and, he complained, they did not believe him when he "Spread wholesome falshood [*sic*] thro' the nation." In a passage clearly presaging M'Fingal's speeches, Gage ironically made himself ridiculous by his charges that the patriots had treated badly such men as Daniel Leonard, James Rivington, Jonathan Sewall, Nathaniel Mills, and John Hicks. In another passage the colonists must have chuckled over, Trumbull may have used ideas from his "small Poem on the late Battle in the Massachusetts" in making Gage say:

> For did not ev'ry reg'lar run
> As soon as e'er you fired a gun;

> And fearful if they stay'd for sport
> You might by accident be hurt,
> Convey'd themselves with speed away,
> Full twenty miles in half-a-day;
> Raced till their legs were grown so weary
> They'd scarce suffice their weight to carry.

Calling for peace and declaring forgiveness to all except Samuel Adams and John Hancock, Gage proclaimed martial law, wished for return to London, and dismissed the Loyalists:

> And all the tory-refugees
> May now go home whene'er they please;
> We've no occasion for such stuff;
> We've British fools and knaves enough.

"By Thomas Gage . . . A Proclamation" was not the "burlesque on General Gage's victories" which Silas Deane had requested, but it was a clever precursor of the more extended one ridiculing not only the acts of that officer but those of the entire British and Tory side. It proved, first, that the author was capable of writing witty irony in the cause of freedom and, second, that he had the courage to publicly ridicule the British, as it was the first time in a published poetic satire that he had portrayed a Briton as a bumbling clown. This jaunty attitude probably played a large part in making the parody such a success that it was republished the next month as an eight-page pamphlet with the title *A New Proclamation*. The step from the parody to the famous mock-epic was short. J. Hammond Trumbull noted at the end of his hand-written copy of the bogus proclamation that "out of" it "naturally grew the first two cantos of 'McFingal,'" a thesis he developed more fully in *The Origin of M'Fingal*.[21]

III   *The Composition of the Mock Epic*

The low morale of the country was an important factor among those leading to the composition of *M'Fingal*. The prevalence of fear and gloom even before Lexington and Concord is verified by Trumbull himself in a letter to Adams or Howe: "We have many of the 'fearful & unbelieving brood' whose imagination is filled with scarecrows, & who dr[ead] much of hangings, confiscations, royal standards, fleets, Armies/ 'Gun, drum, trumpet, blunderbuss and thunder.'/ These people have somehow or other had a revelation, that all the Americans are Cowards, & our Enemies invincible." He described the "prodigies" reported in New Haven, ones such as meteors, drums in the air, the reading of the Bible from the sky, a talking cow, "Apparitions, scriechowls & deathwatches."[22] In such times, copies of the Connecticut *Courant* containing the burlesque proclamation probably reached his friends at the Continental Congress in Philadelphia; and they, knowing his satiric and comic gifts, liking the poem's tone and the ridicule of the British, and seeing the desperate need to hearten many colonials, asked him to write a longer humorous piece.

Trumbull himself testified to the part played by his friends in initiating *M'Fingal*. In 1785, he wrote to the Marquis de Chastellux that he had composed a poem "at the instigation of some of the leading members of the first Congress";[23] and in the "Memoir" of 1820 he said he had written it "at the solicitation of some of his friends in" that body.[24] He provided more specific information in a letter to Silas Deane on October 20, 1775, in which he reminded the recipient of his earlier request for a mock account of Gage's campaigns and said the project had remained in his thoughts. He had made several unsatisfactory attempts at writing the desired burlesque, he said, and had shown them to some friends, who had advised him "to turn the whole into some consistent form & go on with it."[25] From this statement, it appears that Trumbull may have had a substantial amount of work done on a satiric poem before he received a directive late in August or early in September which resulted in the first part of *M'Fingal*.

Information about this order and other facts concerning *M'Fingal* is contained in a hitherto unknown statement by Trumbull's son-in-law, William Woodbridge, one presumably based upon conversations with the author. This account is found in a note at the end of an address Woodbridge gave in Detroit. According to it, Humphreys, under the direction of the Boston group of patriots, wrote Trumbull a letter, and Woodbridge relates how critical it was to the composition of *M'Fingal*:

By this communication Mr. Trumbull was authoritatively admonished that the cause of freedom was in danger. That appalled by the vast power, and the angry tone of Great Britain, the country was sinking into despondency, that something must be attempted, and that quickly, to rouse its spirit, and to excite and elevate its latent energies! The letter concluded with a peremptory order, that he should forthwith prepare something to dispel the melancholy that overspread the patriot cause, that he must write something to "set the people laughing."

Following this mandatory direction, Mr. Trumbull immediately commenced his Hudibrastic Epic, Mc Fingal; . . . "No invoice of goods," (using the emphatic words of Judge Trumbull to the writer of this note) "was ever more truly *made out and sent to order*," than were the parts thus published, of Mc Fingal. . . .[26]

From this speech by Woodbridge, it is evident that those of the Boston group who were in Philadelphia sent an order through Humphreys to Trumbull which he responded to by composing the first part of *M'Fingal.*

With this statement of Woodbridge to complement other accounts, it is possible to trace most of the steps in the origin of Trumbull's most famous poem from his unfinished lines on "the late Battle in the Massachusetts" and Silas Deane's request for "a burlesque on General Gage's victories"[27] to "By Thomas Gage . . . A Proclamation" and unfinished humorous sketches, thence to the reading of the bogus proclamation by Trumbull's Congressional friends and the solicitation, or order, for a longer comic poem ridiculing the British, and finally to the writing of *M'Fingal.* When Trumbull put his pen to paper, he could borrow from his entire recent satiric work, and especially from the comic proclamation, from which he took approximately fifty lines.[28] In September and the first part of October, he labored at his task, composing the long original first canto.

When the strenuous work of writing was over, Trumbull next corresponded with his friends in Philadelphia. He sent the poem to Deane with the request that the latter do with it as he pleased except to leave the style as it was and, if he showed the poem to others, to tell no one except John Adams who the author was. What Deane may have replied to Trumbull about the printing is unknown because only a small fragment remains of his letter to the poet on December 7, 1775. What Adams wrote, however, is available: "It is excellent, and perhaps the more so for being misterious [*sic*]. It wants explanatory Notes as much as Hudibrass [*sic*]—I can't conjecture the Characters either of Honorius or Mc Fingal."[29] Trumbull replied, "As to its being mysterious, as you term it, you know Sir an affected mysteriousness is often a good artifice for exciting the Curiosity of the Public, who are always pleased to have an opportunity of applying fictitious Characters & discovering latent allusions."[30] In response to Adams's other point, he commented: "As to explanatory Notes, the piece I am sensible would want many more than I have given it, in all those places, where personal Characters & particular Allusions are introduced; beyond that the Reader should for me, be welcome to his own guesses."

Publication of the first canto followed quickly, but the last parts were not composed and printed for over six years. Liking the portion which they had received, Deane and Adams had it printed in Philadelphia late in 1775 and published early in 1776. That part, designed "to set the people laughing," was 1389 lines, not quite half of the completed version; but the author already had done work beyond the first section, having formed the entire plan, outlined part of the third canto, and written part of the fourth.[31] At the urging of Humphreys, according to Woodbridge,[32] Trumbull completed the poem in 1782 after he had removed to Hartford. He revised and composed from January to April, dividing the first canto into two and completing the third and fourth cantos.[33] Then in September the finished poem of 3282 lines was published by Hudson and Goodwin.

Trumbull's intention or "design," as he called it, was somewhat different in 1782 from what it had been seven years earlier. In his reply to the Marquis de Chastellux in 1785, he says he attempted to describe in poetry as impartially as he could the struggle for American independence, "with a particular description of the characters and manners of the times, interspersed with anecdotes, which no history would probably record or display...."[34] This statement fits very well the completed poem of 1782 but not the first canto of 1775, for the aim in the latter is more accurately stated in two letters. To Deane he wrote on October 20, 1775, "one main view I had, was to record a few of the most inveterate enemies of our Country, whom I should wish to see otherwise gibbeted up than in my verse." But what seems to be the fullest and most accurate explanation of his plan was given by him on November 14, 1775, in answer to a letter from Adams dated nine days earlier:

To Expose a number of the principal Villains of the day, to ridicule the high blustering menaces & great expectations of the Tory party, & to burlesque the achievements of our ministerial Heroes, civil, ecclesiastical & military, was my whole plan. This could be done with more spirit in dialogue than plain narration, & by a mixture of Irony & Sarcasm under various Characters & different Styles, than in an unvaried harangue in the Author's own person. Nor is it a small beauty in any production of this kind, to paint the manners of the age. For these purposes, the Description of a Townmeeting & its Harangues, appeared the best Vehicle of the Satire. Had there been any one grand Villain, whose Character & History would have answered exactly, I should have made use of him & his real name, as freely as I have the names of others. But I could think of no *One*, & therefore substituted a fictitious Character, of a Scotch Tory Expectant, which I hope is not drawn so illy, but that the world might find hundreds perhaps to whom it might be properly applied. The other Speaker has properly speaking no Character drawn, & no actions ascribed to him. He is any one whose Sentiments are agreeable to his Speeches.

The Picture of the Townmeeting is drawn from the life, & with as proper lights, shades & Colouring as I could give it, & is I fancy no bad likeness.

This, then, was Trumbull's "design" in that portion of *M'Fingal* which was published in 1776.[35]

When he began writing *M'Fingal*, Trumbull aimed at the high burlesque rather than the low. There are several evidences of this fact. First, when he wrote to Silas Deane on May 27, 1775, he suggested that the style of *The Dunciad* might be better than that of *Hudibras*. Second, he said to De Chastellux in 1785 that he had aimed at the high burlesque. And last, there is Joel Barlow's preface to the London edition of 1792 in which the point is made. Because Barlow lived for a time in Trumbull's house in Hartford during the 1780's, he must have become familiar with his host's ideas about his recently completed poem and could speak with authority.

IV *Influences upon* M'Fingal

Though Trumbull was aiming for the high burlesque, *M'Fingal* resembles *Hudibras* in several ways. Like the great English mock epic, it attacks persons; it includes a knight and a squire;

it contains the "mixture of Irony & Sarcasm"[36] which Trumbull admired in Butler; and it uses the octosyllabic couplet, unusual rhymes, and double rhymes. Nearly one-sixth of the couplets have double rhymes, used for humorous effect. They sometimes rival Butler's for cleverness: "dozy"—"idiocy," "submission"—"addition," "atrabilious"—"peccadilloes," and "Erie, or"—"Superior."

In addition, there are over twenty examples of resemblances or borrowings mentioned by J. Hammond Trumbull in his annotated copy of Nathaniel Patten's 1782 edition. In the resemblances, no direct indebtedness is claimed; but passages from *Hudibras* usually are cited. In seven instances, there is an assertion of demonstrable influence: on the gift of prophecy, on guns which miss the mark, on the justification for lying, on Caligula, on the characterization of the Commonwealth, on the owl paraded around Rome, and on an upside-down empire.[37] In the last of these, *M'Fingal* reads, "Whose crupper had o'ertopp'd his head./ You've push'd and turn'd the whole world up-/ Side down, and got yourselves at top." The comparable passage in *Hudibras* is, "Which now had almost got the upper-/ Hand of his head, for want of crupper." One passage in the 1782 edition was so close to *Hudibras* that the author altered it in 1820. Canto I, lines 63-64 read, "Nor only saw he all that was/ But much that never came to pass." In *Hudibras,* similar lines are "He could foretel whats'ever was,/ By consequence to come to pass." For the 1820 edition Trumbull altered his lines to read, "Nor only saw he all that could be,/ But much that never was, nor would be."

Conversant with other English authors of the seventeenth and eighteenth centuries, Trumbull may have been influenced by a number of them. From Prior could come "a kind of easy elegant humour & natural description."[38] Trumbull himself said he sought to imitate Churchill and Swift in his Hudibrastic poems; and he seems principally indebted to Churchill, particularly for the verse patterns and movement of *The Ghost.* In a passage describing qualities he himself strove for, Trumbull wrote: "Churchill aims at sprightliness & vivacity of imagination. His thoughts flow rapidly, & the expression is bold and glowing. The style often bears a nearer resemblance to the Horatian Odes, than to the Poetry from which it takes its name. Indeed this

Style is capable of most of the Beauties of the higher kinds of Poetry." And from Swift probably stemmed the use of humor in description, of combining a conversational style with irony, both of which he credited that British author with having introduced into English poetry.

In addition to the references to historical volumes in the poem, there are numerous allusions to the Bible and to various literary works. Those to the Bible run over forty in number, almost all being from the Old Testament. There are several allusions or references to mock epics, but there are many more to epics, principally—in that order of frequency—to those by Milton, Homer, and Virgil. There are many to ancient authors and to Classical mythology, but there are fewer to more recent works and authors, and these are to ballads. References are to the British Samuel Johnson, Bunyan, Shakespeare, Swift, Thomas Tickell, Edmund Waller, Gray, Prior, General Burgoyne, and Sir Walter Scott; and to the Americans Jonathan Sewall and Cotton Mather. These many allusions give a decidedly literary cast to *M'Fingal*.

The use of a Scotch Tory as M'Fingal has puzzled many readers. Trumbull never explained his choice, but he may well have had three ideas in mind. First, he found the "machinery"[39] of the second sight, reputedly possessed by the Highlanders, advantageous because it would enable him to use the device of prophecy found in some epics. Second, the Scottish members of Parliament supported the ministry in repressive measures against the colonies, and only two voted to repeal the Stamp Act.[40] And, third, however rebellious the Scots may have been at home, they generally were Tories in the colonies, particularly in the Carolinas. As Lossing has pointed out, Jefferson referred in the original draft of the Declaration of Independence to "'Scotch and foreign mercenaries.'"[41]

V *Influence of* M'Fingal

An estimate of the effectiveness of *M'Fingal* as propaganda necessarily is only approximate. The inevitable comparison with Thomas Paine's *Common Sense* and *The Crisis* shows Trumbull's work at a disadvantage, for it was less partisan, it contained many literary allusions which were meaningless to those with little schooling, and poetry was a form less popular than the essay. It seems likely that the influence of *M'Fingal* was felt most among the educated. In this group it could have affected the choice of those who were wavering between the opposing camps, and it gave both assurance and a weapon to the literate patriots. For them, it probably had a value not foreseen by anyone when the request or "order" was sent to Trumbull—that value consisted in its possessing literary stature sufficient to remind readers of Butler's mock epic. Being of such quality, *M'Fingal* helped rid the patriots of their feeling of cultural inferiority, a mighty service not only in 1776 but also in 1782, when the problems of independence loomed closer. Desperately needing something to bolster morale, the patriots welcomed an author who was favorably compared with eminent English writers.

As the records tell us, the satire was esteemed by the revolutionaries in both its 1776 and 1782 editions. On February 21, 1776, Abigail Adams wrote to her husband that "If Mack Fingal [*sic*] is published be so good as to send it."[42] On July 25 of the same year Enoch Hale, brother of Nathan Hale, recorded his purchase of *M'Fingal* for a shilling.[43] In 1782, although General Cornwallis had surrendered and the war was nearly over, copies of the recently published complete *M'Fingal* were favorably received for their combination of patriotic and literary merit. Both Jeremiah Wadsworth and Humphreys wrote about it to General Nathanael Greene,[44] who did not receive his copy until December.[45] He knew Trumbull personally and spoke of the high regard in which he and others held the poet.[46] On September 29, 1782, he wrote to Trumbull that "Many people of this Country wish to get you to become a settler here. Governor Mathews desird [*sic*] me to write you on the subject. Men of taste and genius are much courted and encouraged by the principal Inhabitants."[47] Other leaders also welcomed the patriotic poem. Aaron Burr wrote to Jeremiah Wadsworth, "I am really obliged to you for Mc Fingal. I have read it more than once with great pleasure."[48] Madison wrote about the stir it made in Philadelphia and sent copies to Edmund Randolph,[49] Governor Benjamin Harrison,[50] and Edmund Pendleton.[51] Humphreys carried a copy from the author to Thomas Jefferson. John Jay was acquainted with it and referred to it.[52] Washington owned a copy, which later was in the Huth Library in England but is now back in America in the Chapin Library at Williams College.

Any satisfaction which Trumbull may have derived from the popularity of *M'Fingal* was lessened by the fact that satire often was thought inferior or immoral. Even John Adams later urged his former law student to use his "veins of Poetry of Superior kinds,"[53] that is, the epic. Trumbull wisely declined any attempt at a form to which he did not feel equal, despite his ambition to write in the "sublime" or "pathetic" style.[54] But what irritated Trumbull was the carping criticism that satire was sinful. In January 1783 he recorded some of his thoughts in an unpublished essay called "On Satirical Productions."[55] Since the most important detractors presumably were clergymen, he met them on their own ground and cited the fable of Jotham, Elijah's speech to Baal's prophets, the Book of Job, and many other examples to buttress his point that the Bible has "many Passages ... which have never been excelled by the most witty Satirist of antient or modern ages." Adding a few remarks at the end of the esssay, he mentioned examples of irony in Scripture also. Though he hoped he could silence his critics, he recognized that arguing with those "who are determined not to be convinced" was futile.

VI *Canto I   The Town-meeting,* A.M.

Trumbull opens the first canto with mockery of British might as displayed at Lexington and Concord. Then he describes Squire M'Fingal, the representative of the Tories and the possessor of second-sight, making his way to his home town. In a jocular reference to the reputed gift of prophecy, the author writes:

> For any man with half an eye
> What stands before him can espy;
> But optics sharp it needs, I ween,
> To see what is not to be seen. (6)

These frequently quoted couplets are often mistakenly attributed to *Hudibras.*

Though endowed with prophetic powers, M'Fingal is not

always helpful to his cause and its adherents. As the author tells it:

> But as some muskets so contrive it,
> As oft to miss the mark they drive at,
> And though well aim'd at duck or plover,
> Bear wide, and kick their owners over:
> So fared our 'Squire, whose reas'ning toil
> Would often on himself recoil,
> And so much injured more his side,
> The stronger arguments he applied;
> As old war-elephants, dismay'd,
> Trod down the troops they came to aid,
> And hurt their own side more in battle,
> Than less and ordinary cattle. (8)

Because M'Fingal arrives late at the town meeting, the Whig leader Honorius begins speaking first. He utilizes the popular idea that political states, like people, have their various ages; and he charges that Great Britain is now grown old and has lost her senses, even claiming in the Declaratory Act to be all-powerful. In his effort to reassure his countrymen by his ridicule of England, Trumbull draws a satiric comparison:

> "As madmen, straw who long have slept on,
> Style themselves Jupiter and Neptune:
> So Britain in her airs so flighty,
> Now took a whim to be Almighty;
> Urg'd on to desperate heights of frenzy,
> Affirm'd her own Omnipotency." (14)

In his accusations, Honorius insists that Britain has been deaf to pleas and has sent Gage, a prime liar, to Boston. Though that officer bungles his falsehoods, he is a threat:

> "Yet fools are often dangerous enemies;
> As meanest reptiles are most venomous:
> Nor e'er could Gage, by craft or prowess,
> Have done a whit more mischief to us;
> Since he began th' unnat'ral war,
> The work his masters sent him for." (19)

Having castigated Gage, Honorius condemns the "Tory expect-
ants," the "dastard race" of those clergymen, lawyers, merchants,
and judges

> "...who long have sold
> Their souls and consciences for gold;
> Who wish to stab their country's vitals,
> Could they enjoy surviving titles." (20)

When M'Fingal gives a signal, his adherents, who follow him
"like files of geese," make an uproar. M'Fingal then begins his
first speech, which is full of unintended irony. Charging that
the Whigs are too stupid to understand logic, he defends the
Anglicans:

> "Have not our High-church Clergy made it
> Appear from Scriptures, which ye credit,
> That right divine from heaven was lent
> To kings, that is, the Parliament,
> Their subjects to oppress and teaze,
> And serve the devil when they please?" (23-24)

He continues, naming clergy:

> "Have ye not heard from Parson Walter
> Much dire presage of many a halter?
> What warnings had ye of your duty,
> From our old rev'rend Sam. Auchmuty;
> From priests of all degrees and metres,
> T' our fag-end man, poor Parson Peters?" (24)

M'Fingal advises the colonials to bear silently the plague of
modern kings sent by God, and he extols the reasoning powers
of "scribblers" on the Tory side, such as Massachusettensis.

In a passage appealing to religious sentiment, Honorius chal-
lenges the Tory:

> " 'Twas then belike," Honorius cried,
> "When you the public fast defied,
> Refused to heaven to raise a prayer,
> Because you'd no connections there." (31)

Replying, M'Fingal asks whether heaven had sent Judge Peter Oliver, an "ignoramus"; Sewall, a "wit of water-gruel"; and Nat. Ray Thomas, the "Marshfield blunderer"; Thomas Hutchinson; or Treasurer Harrison Gray. Then Honorius reminds the Tories how Hutchinson has lied—a fact that does not disturb M'Fingal, who defends all brother Ananiases:

> Quoth he, "For lies and promise-breaking,
> Ye need not be in such a taking:
> For lying is, we know and teach,
> The highest privilege of speech;
> The universal Magna Charta,
> To which all human race is party." (35)

After excusing lies further, M'Fingal calls for a dinner recess.

The first canto, which establishes the poem as a mock epic, is distinguished from the third and fourth cantos by the greater intensity of its opposition to the British and the Tories. The poem tells of inglorious military expeditions, lists opposition heroes, and includes a debate, which is carried on at a town meeting. To ridicule the opposition, Trumbull employs scorn and occasionally invective, as when he calls Parson Samuel Peters a "fag-end man." Indicative also of the author's seriousness are the many references to the Bible and the few to the *Iliad*, the *Odyssey*, the *Aeneid*, *Paradise Lost*, and *Fingal*. Sometimes he makes a sharp satiric stroke by echoing a biblical passage, as he does with Acts 17:28 when he writes "In them, who made you Tories, seeing/ You lived and moved and had your being." In the first canto also is the one satirical reference to the metaphysical divines with whom he had been battling for over five years. Contributing to the humor in a lighter way are over one hundred fifty double rhymes, a greater number than in any of the other cantos. The first canto, as well as the second one, reflects strongly the patriotic involvement of Trumbull in Boston and New Haven.

VII *Canto II The Town-meeting*, P.M.

Canto II opens with mock-heroic lines about the sun which are reminiscent of the "Epithalamion" and then goes to the dinner:

(Nor shall we, like old Homer, care
To versify their bill of fare)
Each active party, feasted well,
Throng'd in, like sheep, at sound of bell;
With equal spirit took their places,
And meeting oped with three *Oh Yesses*. ([41])

M'Fingal rises and calls the Whigs ungrateful. In another un-
knowingly ironical speech, he cites the colonials' supposed debt
to Charles I, Archbishop Laud, soldiers, governors, judges, and
clergymen. In addition, he maintains the British "'brought all
felons in the nation/ To help you on in population.'" He derides
patriotism and insists "'That self is still, in either faction,/ The
only principle of action'"; and he questions doing anything for
posterity. M'Fingal then calls the Whigs cowards, reminds them
of British military might, and, incongruously, mentions that the
British used Indians against the colonials as well as instigated
slave revolts.

Honorius answers the challenge on British military strength by
citing Gage's proclamation. M'Fingal makes the ridiculous
answer that Providence chooses its own instruments:

"To pay a tax, at Peter's wish,
His chief cashier was once a fish;
An ass, in Balaam's sad disaster,
Turn'd orator and saved his master;
A goose, placed sentry on his station,
Preserved old Rome from desolation;
An English bishop's cur of late
Disclosed rebellions 'gainst the state;
So frogs croak'd Pharaoh to repentance,
And lice delay'd the fatal sentence:
And heaven can ruin you at pleasure,
By Gage, as soon as by a Caesar." (54-55)

With unwitting irony M'Fingal cites Colonel Nesbit's tarring
and feathering of a farmer, Colonel Alexander Leslie's ineffective
trip to Salem, Gage's statement that he tried to avert civil war,
the battle of Lexington, the actions of Abijah White, and the
British soldiers who mistook "whizzing beetles" for whizzing
bullets. With second sight M'Fingal foresees gallows for Whigs;
the sack of cities; the arrival of the British navy and its thieving

of provisions; the bombast of Gage, Admiral Samuel Graves, and Captain James Wallace; the coming of prodigies; and "new setts/ Of home-made Earls in Massachusetts."

Honorius responds with a stirring call for liberty: " 'Tis Freedom calls! the raptured sound/ The Apalachian hills rebound.' " Scornfully, Honorius addresses the faint-hearted:

> "And ye, whose souls of dastard mould
> Start at the bravery of the bold;
> To love your country who pretend,
> Yet want all spirit to defend. (79)

Such persons Honorius advises to go home and hide behind the aprons of their "more heroic wives." Tumult breaks out, and "Plumed Victory" sits on the pulpit-canopy ready to join the winning side. But suddenly a shout comes from outside, and the meeting breaks up. Like a knight and his squire, M'Fingal and the constable sally outdoors.

Written originally as part of Canto I, the second canto resembles the first in most respects and differs in only a few. It includes such mock-epic conventions as a meal, Plumed Victory, a knight and squire, omens, speeches, and innocuous battles. It makes its points with irony and invective. It contains many allusions to the Bible and several to epics, particularly to the *Iliad*. Proportionately, it contains fewer double rhymes than the first canto. It differs in including a pun (on Lord North's name) and in referring to two mock epics—the *Batrachomuomachia* and *Hudibras*. And in Canto 2 there are verses Washington may have thought particularly apt, for in his copy of the Hudson and Goodwin edition there are penciled double lines which he likely made beside "What has posterity done for us,/ That we, least they their rights should lose,/ Should trust our necks to gripe of noose?"

VIII *Canto III The Liberty Pole*

The third canto differs considerably from the first two. Trumbull followed the earlier recommendation of Silas Deane to use different styles in each part, and he also heeded the advice of those friends such as Humphreys who urged him to complete the poem as literature by filling the canto with literary allusions and echoes. Furthermore, although he had outlined parts of

Canto III by the first part of October 1775, he could scarcely have written them as they now stand. For example, the speech of M'Fingal at the liberty pole, around which a noisy crowd has gathered, was startlingly different from his earlier bumbling and ridiculous harangues. With the Revolution almost over, the poet endorsed the views of the American upper classes toward the lower ones by evincing little sympathy for the social revolution taking place along with the political one. M'Fingal's speech condemning the mob lacks the irony of those in the first two cantos; and we recognize the difference between the philosophy of "life, liberty, and the pursuit of happiness" in the Declaration of Independence and that of "life, liberty, and property" incorporated in the colonial charters and in the Constitution.

M'Fingal, in fact, at first sounds as straightforward as Honorius when he addresses the patriots as "dupes to every factious rogue/ And tavern-prating demagogue" and when he charges that, for them, liberty "Is but for crimes a patent license." He accuses them of hypocritical selfishness when he says they "Dispute and pray and fight and groan/ For public good, and mean [their] own." And Honorius actually voices the author's own sentiments when he observes,

> "And when by clamours and confusions,
> Your freedom's grown a public nuisance,
> Cry 'Liberty,' with powerful yearning,
> As he does 'Fire!' whose house is burning;
> Though he already has much more
> Than he can find occasion for." (90)

Continuing, M'Fingal scornfully derides the weakness of Congress and the election of tradesmen as legislators. Gradually he works into his old habit of unintentional irony, but not before the author has condemned weak central government and paper money. Returning to his former style, M'Fingal alludes to North, the Earl of Bute, and Governor Tryon and to the mobs in New York which have done work cheered by the patriots.

But the Whigs grow tired of M'Fingal's harangue, and a fight breaks out. The description of the ensuing battle parodies the epic accounts, among them that between the Lapithae and Centaurs in the twelfth book of Ovid's *Metamorphoses*. M'Fingal cries " 'King George' " three times, draws his sword, and enters

the melee. A powerful Whig with a spade bests him in combat
with "a blow/ Tremendous on his rear below." When the supporting Tories have vanished, and M'Fingal and the constable
are caught, the constable is hoisted to the top of the liberty
pole, where he, like Socrates in *The Clouds,* thinks more clearly,
and renounces Toryism. M'Fingal, however, stands "heroic as
a mule," and argues that punishment will merely "provoke"
offenders, as "No man e'er felt the halter draw,/ With good
opinion of the law." A bench of justice is established, and
M'Fingal and his aid are quickly sentenced to tarring and feathering, with a subsequent ride through town. As in a description
in Claudian, tar streams down from M'Fingal's head. After the
feathering, he outdoes several rival literary figures:

> Not Maia's son, with wings for ears,
> Such plumage round his visage wears;
> Nor Milton's six-wing'd angel gathers
> Such superfluity of feathers.
> Now all complete appears our 'Squire,
> Like Gorgon or Chimaera dire;
> Nor more could boast on Plato's plan
> To rank among the race of man,
> Or prove his claim to human nature,
> As a two-legg'd unfeather'd creature. (115)

After the ride through town, the two men are brought back to
the pole and stuck to it. M'Fingal then speaks and reveals that
his prophetic sight predicts a Whig victory. He concludes by
directing the constable to call a Tory meeting.

Distinguishing the third canto are the liberty pole, which,
like the town meeting, was a New England institution; the fewer
biblical references; the increased number of literary allusions;
the seven references to Milton; the smaller number of double
rhymes; and the one triple rhyme in the poem—"trouble ye"—
"jubilee." It continues the mock-epic conventions, of course,
one of which is a ridiculous individual combat. All in all, the
canto has a decidedly more literary cast than the first two.

IX *Canto IV The Vision*

The fourth canto opens with an appropriate mock-heroic
description:

Now Night came down, and rose full soon
That patroness of rogues, the Moon;
Beneath whose kind protecting ray,
Wolves, brute and human, prowl for prey.
The honest world all snored in chorus,
While owls and ghosts and thieves and Tories,
Whom erst the mid-day sun had awed,
Crept from their lurking holes abroad. ([121])

The "Tory pandemonium" meets in the cellar of M'Fingal, in which he addresses the assemblage from a turnip bin. With his second sight he perceives John Malcolm, Governor Tryon's aid, who does most of the prophesying. Referring to actual events of the war, more than in the third, the author, through Malcolm's words, cites patriot victories and pays graceful compliments to Washington and to General Greene, his correspondent and friend. The defeats of Burgoyne and Cornwallis are announced along with the ultimate patriot victory. The vision ends when the constable announces that the Whigs are coming, and M'Fingal makes "good his rear" with an ignominious exit and leaves for Boston. This craven action fittingly concludes the poem.

The fourth canto has the deepest literary hue of all the cantos. The longest of the four divisions, it has nearly twice as many literary allusions, many being to Classical mythology, to Virgil, and to Milton. It has fewer double rhymes than either of the first two cantos. It is so impartial that it and number three must have been in Trumbull's mind when he wrote to De Chastellux that he had tried to point out the faults of both sides in the Revolution.

X *Editions*

One of the most popular American poems, *M'Fingal* has had numerous editions. For many years its identification with patriotism and the unity of the nation brought republication in times of national crisis. The period of the Constitutional Convention, the neutrality controversy during the French Revolution, the War of 1812, and the Civil War all saw renewed interest. From 1810 to 1816, for instance, there were eight known editions. In his "Memoir" Trumbull estimated that there had been in excess of "thirty different impressions" between 1782 and 1820, although research to date has discovered only twenty-four. Cowie lists twenty-three of them; to these should be added the one issued by William Slade, Jr., in Middlebury, Vermont.[56] Later editions which may be added to Cowie's total list are Parrington's *The Connecticut Wits* (1926); Edwin T. Bowden's edition called *The Satiric Poems of John Trumbull: The Progress of Dulness and M'Fingal* (1962); the reprints of the *Poetical Works* by Scholarly Press (1968), Reprint House International (1968), and Adler (1968); and the Burt Franklin reprint of the *Poetical Works* as edited by A. H. Nason in 1922 (1968).

It is now possible to say definitely that Barlow was the editor of the London edition of 1792. This fact had been assumed, but no conclusive proof had been adduced. Trumbull wrote on a flyleaf of his copy that it was a gift from the editor, but he did not specify who the editor was.[57] Howard states that Joel Barlow edited the 1792 *M'Fingal,*[58] as does Charles B. Todd.[59] Apparently scholars have relied upon Franklin B. Dexter, whose attribution of the editorship to Barlow is noted by Jacob Blanck,[60] but Dexter does not list any source. Barlow himself states his role in a letter he wrote to James Watson from London on August 2, 1792: "I take the liberty to send to you two copies of your favourite Poem, M^c-Fingal. To which I have written Notes & a Preface. I would be much obliged to you to keep one for yourself & send the other to Friend Trumbull, for whom I cherish the most tender regard. Don't let him know it came from me & nor that I was the editor."[61]

Trumbull was disturbed by the preface and notes in the edition published by his friend Barlow. The preface to the New York edition of 1795, the only impression between 1782 and 1820 "published with the permission, or even the knowledge of the writer,"[62] stated that because the London edition "was published to answer the purposes of a party, and the Editor has taken the liberty to misrepresent the views of the Author, the preface and such of the notes as were inserted for that purpose, are here omitted. This is done at the request of the author, with whose permission, this edition is offered to the American public."[63] In his own copy of the London edition Trumbull showed his displeasure with the notes added by crossing out words, phrases, paragraphs, and sometimes entire notes. On page twenty-three, for example, he crossed out "a paper which

answered very well to its title, it being filled with those im-
positions and falsehoods, which are deemed necessary to the
support of Royalty, in any country where printing is tolerated."
And on page 130 he drew lines through "Vive la Revolution!"

The pirating of *M'Fingal* in 1782 by Nathaniel Patten and
Bavil Webster gave impetus to the successful drive for copyright laws. The Hudson and Goodwin edition, on which Trumbull ran the financial risk for the 2,024 copies, appeared in early
September 1782; and the pirated editions, according to their
advertisement, were published on December 28 of the same
year. In the Connecticut *Courant* for January 7, 1783, as Cowie
has noted,[64] Trumbull bitingly attacked the piracy of literary
works. He pointed out that the author had all the labor of composing and all the risks of publishing without any reasonable
hope of "pecuniary compensation." His disappointment over the
injustice to a writer is clear in passages such as the following:

The moment his work has gained the public attention, he finds it
reprinted by another, and all efforts, of slander, advertisement, sub-
scription, and every other ungenerous method taken to prevent the
sale of his edition. Even his own subscribers forget their obligation,
and suffer many hundred copies printed perhaps only to satisfy their
subscriptions, to lie on hand as waste paper, while they wholly
neglect their engagements and perhaps purchase the meaner and
therefore cheaper edition of the mercenary invader of his property.
While amid the calumnies with which his enemies are overwhelming
his reputation, he has this sole consolation that his whole labours
have been employed only to enrich the man, who had used every
art to injure and defraud him.

This protest by Trumbull and concerted efforts by him and his
friends had their desired effect, for in the same month the state
legislature passed a copyright law upon "the petition of several
literary gentlemen," obviating the need for a memorial which
Noah Webster had prepared.[65]

XI   *Fame of Poem and Author*

The fame of the poem made its author something of a celebrity. When William Loughton Smith of Carolina was touring the

North,[66] he noted that Trumbull was at a dinner given by Jeremiah Wadsworth. The Marquis de Chastellux wrote from France proffering his compliments on *M'Fingal*,[67] and J. P. Brissot de Warville mentioned its author favorably.[68] Eminent foreigners sometimes sought him out, as did the South American general Francisco de Miranda, who came to Hartford from Wethersfield on August 8, 1784, to call on the distinguished patriot. The next day Trumbull and his family returned the visit, and the two men discussed Classical and recent foreign literature.[69]

Despite Trumbull's delight in incongruity, he may have had mixed feelings about having the name of the hero in his best-known work applied to himself, in derision by his opponents and with affection by his friends. In 1801, he was cast as M'Fingal in the scurrilous *Federalism Triumphant in the Steady Habits of Connecticut Alone, Or, The Turnpike Road to a Fortune*. Three years later a young man named Lonson Nash was writing from Stockbridge to William Woodbridge in Ohio praising Juliana Trumbull and identifying her as "a daughter of M'Fingal's."[70] The name apparently was so generally associated with Trumbull that in 1824 a newspaper account of a dinner for him in New York began with "M'Fingal Dinner."[71] The habit persisted for decades, as is clear from a notice of the death of the son Samuel's widow in 1863: "Mrs. Elizabeth Trumbull, who died in Brooklyn, recently at the age of 84, was the daughter-in-law of Judge John Trumbull, one of the famous Hartford wits, and widely known as McFingal."[72]

The renown of the poem was reflected in references to it in newspapers, speeches, and books.[73] It was quoted both by the Federalists and by their opponents during political battles, for each side found neat epigrams to pilfer for political debate. It must have been noticed, of course, that the Federalists sometimes quoted the M'Fingal of Canto III rather than Honorius. Some references to the poem were not political, but private, as was that of Mason Fitch Cogswell, a Hartford physician, who wrote:

> Come then Thou spirit of M'Fingal
> Descend and with Thy influence Tingle
> My every feeling that with ease
> I may describe whate'er I please.[74]

The critical reception of *M'Fingal* has varied considerably over the years, as some examples demonstrate. Because magazines had not become established in America when the poem was first published, the earliest reviews are found not in American but in British periodicals. The *Gentleman's Magazine and Historical Chronicle* merely listed the Almon edition of 1776;[75] and the *Critical Review: or, Annals of Literature* was hostile, calling it "A doggerel rhapsody, extended through forty-four pages, without wit, humour, or any discoverable design."[76] The *Monthly Review; or Literary Journal*, on the other hand, found it praiseworthy: "We here find wit, and humour, and barbarous rhymes, as frequent as in the British Hudibras: nor does the Yankey Poet seem, as far as we may judge from a performance so comparatively small, in any respect, inferior to his predecessor, of merry memory."[77]

When the London (Jordan) edition was published in 1792, the *Critical Review: or, Annals of Literature* condemned the poem as neither "highly humorous [n]or entertaining";[78] but the *Monthly Review; or Literary Journal* lauded it except for "the horrid rhymes, which are still worse than those that debase the witty performance of Butler."[79] In the *Monthly Magazine, and British Register* for August 1798 Elihu Hubbard Smith, an American, averred the poem had "been favourably received in Europe, and . . . read with rapture in America."[80] Finally, in 1825, *Blackwood's Edinburgh Magazine* called it "a Hudibrastic poem of great merit—for doggrel [sic]—rich, bold, and happy."[81]

Judged on the basis of a fairly large sampling, American appraisals remained generally favorable. In a review of the work of Timothy Dwight and Joel Barlow in 1788, the contributor (probably Dr. Lemuel Hopkins) said, "I cannot conclude without adding a remark upon another late production of which *America* boasts, *Mr. Trumbull's M'Fingal*. It is a master piece of its kind, and not inferiour in genuine wit and poetical merit, to *Butler's Hero*."[82] In the next issue the same contributor added more praise. Five years later in *The History of the American Revolution*, David Ramsay stressed the important role Trumbull's mock-heroic poem played in diverting the Americans' attention from their hardships during the long war.[83]

After the turn of the century, some writers came to regard the poem as outdated, but most continued to consider it a significant patriotic literary achievement. In 1803, the *Literary Tablet* extolled it unstintingly,[84] and in 1829 Kettell commended it and noted its importance "for overcoming excessive deference toward England" but qualified his praise by mentioning the part "the time and circumstances" played in promoting its "celebrity."[85] In 1834, when the painter John Trumbull and Theodore Dwight suggested to Elihu White, the poet's son-in-law, that the tombstone bear only the inscription "John Trumbull, author of M'Fingal," the artist "observed that this was honor enough for one man, and wd [*sic*] last as long as time."[86] In the next year Timothy Flint estimated that *M'Fingal* was "in many places hardly inferior to [*Hudibras*]."[87] The poem was lauded in the *Southern Literary Messenger* in 1841,[88] but Edgar Allan Poe condemned it.[89] Rufus Wilmot Griswold called it "much the best imitation of the great satire of Butler that has been written,"[90] and Charles Everest termed it "one of the most useful and acceptable offerings laid upon the altar of liberty."[91] In 1855 the Duyckincks opened their article on Trumbull with the words "The author of *M'Fingal*."[92] In 1856, A. P. Peabody saw merits in the poem and attributed its decline in popularity "to the lack of picturesqueness in the story, and of all elements of permanent interest in its heroes."[93] In 1865, Sheldon referred to De Chastellux's praise and said, "Notwithstanding the opinion of the pompous Marquis, nobody reads 'Mc Fingal.'"[94] Continuing the unfavorable estimate, he cited well-known epigrams and suggested, "Perhaps a few other grains of corn might be picked out of these hundred and seventy pages of chaff." When Sheldon made these comments, he may have been unaware of the new editions of 1860 and 1864.

But, despite some unfavorable criticism, *M'Fingal* could not be ignored or dismissed, as Edmund Stedman has pointed out.[95] Whatever its defects, it was the most popular American poem until Henry Wadsworth Longfellow's *Evangeline* was published in 1847; and its primacy as our best political satire was unchallenged until the *Biglow Papers* came into print. New editions became scarcer, but the poem was anthologized. Twentieth-century critics, such as William Otis,[96] Cowie,[97] Henry Seidel Canby,[98] Bruce Ingham Granger,[99] and Bowden[100] have given accolades to *M'Fingal*; and librarians recently selected it as one of the volumes in a permanent White House "library of books central to the understanding of the American national experience."[101] The position of *M'Fingal* as one of the best books of the Revolutionary era is secure.

CHAPTER 5

"Useful in Public Affairs"

TRUMBULL'S reduced literary production after 1782 was owing to several factors. First, for many years he did not have energy and stamina for prolonged writing because of poor health, as Parrington noted.[1] Never robust, the poet incurred a debilitating illness in the spring of 1780 which left him with two decades of weakness during the very period when he should have been at the height of his powers. In the 1780's, he suffered from "nervous complaints";[2] in the 1790's, he underwent several extremely difficult years—in fact, he declined physically so much that Lemuel Hopkins wrote to Oliver Wolcott, Jr., that Trumbull would "within a year or two, quit the 'visible diurnal sphere.'"[3] During the decade he gave up his private law practice as well as municipal and state posts. Only after a severe attack of "tetanus" in 1798 did he begin his recovery of moderately good health.

Some other factors affecting any possible belletristic production were the necessity to make a living, his political activities, and his personal disappointments. Despite his father's comparative wealth, the son received no support after leaving college.[4] As a politician, he was elected a Common Councilman in Hartford annually from 1784 (five years earlier than has been thought)[5] through 1791 and elected an alderman in 1792. In that year and in 1800 and 1801 he was elected to the state legislature; and in 1793 and in 1800 he received a substantial, though insufficient, number of votes for the House of Representatives.[6] He also was state's attorney from Hartford from 1789 to 1795.

From 1801 to 1819 he was a judge of the Connecticut Supreme Court, and from 1808 to 1819 a judge of the Superior Court of

Errors. During his judgeship he considered it would be unethical for him to write on political issues. One scholar has said that "he never experienced any real disappointment or profound hopelessness,"[7] but this statement is inaccurate. Of the seven children born to him and his wife, three died in infancy or early childhood; the oldest son was shiftless[8] and a drain on his father's resources; and his beloved and promising son Leverett died a year after being graduated from Yale. Trumbull also was frustrated in his hopes for a federal appointment, and he was nearly impoverished by being turned out of his state judgeship in 1819.

I *Trumbull in Collaboration*

Most of Trumbull's later writing done in collaboration was in verse, but there were two instances of prose, both of which involved Washington. The more important of these was "A Circular Letter . . . to the Governors of the several States," which was sent out in June 1783, as a last message from General Washington to the governors and their legislators before he left his post as head of the army. In it, he listed four points he regarded as indispensable to the continued existence of the United States as a nation: a permanent federal government under a single chief executive; the discharge of all debts to soldiers, officers, and creditors; the institution of a defense force; and a spirit of good will among the citizens which would allow priority to the common good.

Dissatisfied with Humphreys's draft developing these ideas, Washington turned to Trumbull in May 1783, when the latter stopped at the headquarters in Newburgh to meet Barlow for a trip to Philadelphia designed to promote the sale of their books. Depending upon hearsay, Noah Webster some years later wrote that Barlow and Trumbull had composed the long letter and that Washington had revised it;[9] Trumbull, however, has given the true account in his own handwriting. This disclosure of his role in correcting the circular we owe partly to excessive heat for two weeks in July 1805, and, as he expressed it, "to the decided attention, which my numerous companions in the Bedstead thought it their duty to pay to a Connecticut Judge."[10] Both these facts contributed to the fatigue and irritability he felt when he returned briefly to Hartford from the judicial circuit and found John Adams's personal letter dated July 8, 1805, one in the series the men exchanged. In the letter, Adams suggested that his correspondent deserved a better position than judge.

Ordinarily, Trumbull kept his ambitions to himself, but, fatigued as he was, he felt irked enough by Adams's suggestion, to write a candid reply, "The *more* & the *higher* must have come from another quarter. My feelings prompt me to put the question, Why was I totally neglected at the first organization of the general Government?" Trumbull then recorded for Adams how General Washington's circular from Newburgh was composed and improved:

Washington had a right certainly, if he pleased, "To scorn the humble Poet of his praise." Indeed his character was too high, to want the aid of eulogies. But he knew me well & was under personal obligations to me—I will mention the principal one. It was wholly owing to me, that his last circular address, on quitting the army, had not been a mere schoolboy declamation, & in some parts absolutely contemptible. [This must be kept to ourselves, & especially from one of my best friends, Col. H.] I happened to be at the Camp, when the thing, such as it was, had been composed by the person hinted at, & was ready for signing. Washington, who had too much good sense to be pleased with it, & too little scholarship to write one for himself, directed it to be submitted to my inspection. I struck out at least half, caused many other passages to be written anew, corrected the whole, & inserted a few sentences of my own, which I leave you to discover by your critical sagacity. All this was sorely against the will of the Draughtsman, who really thought he had produced a perfect model of sublime eloquence. But the General approved of every alteration I proposed.

Adams could "discern nothing of Humphries [*sic*]"[11] in the circular, but he knew his correspondent well enough so that he could identify some passages written by Trumbull. He observed, for example, "There is a turn of keenness in one paragraph—'The People have their choice to make independence a blessing or a curse'—which I impute to you. . . ." The paragraph alluded to indeed seems to show the parallelism, lucidity, and balanced sentences which marked Trumbull's prose style. It warns of the danger that European governments would foment discord among the states and then ends with the passage Adams cited: "For, according to the system of Policy the States shall adopt at this moment, they will stand or fall, and by their confirmation or lapse, it is yet to be decided, whether the Revolution must ultimately be considered as a blessing or a curse: a blessing or a curse, not to the present age alone, for with our fate will the destiny of unborn Millions be involved."[12] Although Washington's ideas did not prevail at once, they did within a few years. Perhaps it is not too much to say that Trumbull's recasting of Humphreys's draft and his addition of sentences of his own increased the cogency of the important last circular letter, which came to be esteemed highly and to be known as "Washington's Legacy."

In another collaboration connected with Washington, Trumbull, Chauncey Goodrich, and Noah Webster composed an address on July 29, 1793, from the citizens of Hartford to President Washington. At the time, France and England had begun hostilities, Washington had issued his proclamation of neutrality, and public opinion was divided over the President's action. Some of his staunchest support lay in Connecticut, where the citizens joyously welcomed him as he traversed the state as part of his New England trip. When he visited Hartford on August 2, Samuel Wyllys delivered the address prepared by the committee, and the President responded. Both speeches were printed in the Connecticut *Courant* for August 19, 1793.[13]

With three articulate men involved in the writing, it is impossible to separate their individual contributions. We may be sure, though, that Trumbull affected the dignified tone, the clarity, and the exactness of expression in the patriotic document. The key paragraph in the address read by Wyllys is the following: "Warmly attached to our government, both by interest and affection, we take the liberty to assure You, that we shall ever stand ready by our utmost exertions, in every legal and constitutional way, to support the just measures of your administration, and to lend our assistance in maintaining the peace and harmony of the States, and opposing the insidious designs of those persons, if there be any so deluded, who may wish to subject the country to foreign influence, and involve it in the horrors of war." Washington could not but be pleased by the loyal support expressed in the message written by the three men.

Trumbull collaborated with Humphreys at least three times

after Washington's letter of June 1783. In their only nonpolitical partnership, the two produced the prologue and epilogue of the drama *The Widow of Malabar*, as Humphreys gracefully acknowledged in his letter dedicating the play to Trumbull. The other joint work involved the struggle for a more powerful national government. In the first of these collaborative efforts, Humphreys sought to ridicule William Williams, a liberal politician from Lebanon, in a verse fable called "The Monkey, Who Shaved Himself and His Friends."[14] Having difficulty with the ending, Humphreys brought it to his collaborator, who, according to J. Hammond Trumbull, immediately supplied the last two couplets. Most of the value in the poem lies in these four lines, which with the swiftness of repartee make the point intended:

> His cheeks dispatch'd—his visage thin
> He cock'd, to shave beneath his chin;
> Drew razor swift as he could pull it,
> And cut from ear to ear his gullet.[15]

In his *Recollections*, S. G. Goodrich credits Trumbull with the last couplet only; but James Hammond Trumbull, using as his source the poet's own marked copy of Humphreys's *Miscellaneous Works*, attributes the last four lines to him.

The other political propaganda on which the two men collaborated also involved Joel Barlow and Lemuel Hopkins. The four men argued for a stronger national government in *The Anarchiad*, which received its name from a bogus poem quoted in a twelve-part series individually titled "American Antiquities, No. I" and so on. Published from October 26, 1786, to September 13, 1787, the articles appeared first in the *New-Haven Gazette, and the Connecticut Magazine*, except for Number XI, which appeared initially in the Connecticut *Courant*.[16] The four friends were stimulated to write by the general unrest in the country during the serious depression following the Revolution. In the sluggish economy, many former soldiers were unemployed, and the debtor class was in the majority. The Articles of Confederation, despite their merits, were not strong enough to provide a firm fiscal policy, and the new nation drifted toward civil strife. Many debtors, fearing the rise of an aristocracy, resented the extra pay given to the former army officers and took it as a sign the social revolution accompanying the political one was in danger. When foreclosures increased in Massachusetts, mobs prevented courts from sitting, and Daniel Shays and others led a "rebellion." In Rhode Island, there was talk of issuing paper money and making it legal tender by an enforcing act. As much greater internal strife seemed imminent, many able men posed the alternatives as being either anarchy or a stronger central government; and among them were the writers soon to be called the "Hartford Wits."

The Anarchiad was a vigorous political satire built on a clever use of a fable. Aimed at demolishing its targets, it incorporated a savage irony along with ridicule, scorn, and derogatory nicknames. Not perfectly consistent in tone, it nevertheless attacked generally the opponents of a strong Constitution with skill, if not with fairness. Its verse is characterized by partisan political articulations rather than by belletristic merit.

Behind the inception of *The Anarchiad* was a letter sent by William Williams of Lebanon to Joseph Hopkins of Waterbury concerning a forthcoming meeting of the Society of the Cincinnati, a fraternal order composed of former patriot officers in the Revolutionary War, whom Williams suspected of having designs on western lands. On the way, the letter was broken open and transcribed; and on October 9, 1786, a slightly inaccurate copy of it appeared in the Connecticut *Courant*, and accompanying it was a burlesque versification of it signed "William Wimble," attributed by Howard[17] to Trumbull but initialed *N* by Noah Webster on his own copy to indicate that he had written it.[18] Williams wrote a letter correcting the printed version and accusing General Samuel H. Parsons, president of the Connecticut Cincinnati, of having had a hand in the pilfering.

A series of letters, many bogus, followed in the Connecticut *Courant* and in the *New-Haven Gazette, and the Connecticut Magazine*, some angry and some humorous; and in one of these the expression "wicked wits" appeared. Then in the issue of October 26 the friends began in the New Haven paper the series called "American Antiquities." With elaborate satire the authors delineated the merits of the supposed realm of King Anarch and provided a vision of the future, which was, of course, the post-Revolutionary period. While most of the numbers incorporated biting irony to expose anti-Federalist proposals such as more paper money, Number X was a straightforward exhortation to the Constitutional Convention, which was about to assemble; and it ended with a firm warning: " 'Ye live united, or divided die,' " a line repeated at the end of the publisher's advertisement for the Luther G. Riggs edition of 1861.

The roles of the various authors are extremely difficult to determine. Probably the general concept of the series was contributed by Humphreys, as Trumbull said in the "Memoir." While in London, Colonel Humphreys had seen the *Rolliad*, a spurious epic containing prophecies about eighteenth-century British political life. All the men presumably were acquainted with the contemporary interest in archaeological excavations in Ohio and the speculations concerning them. On November 16, 1786, when the first two numbers were in print, Humphreys wrote to Washington that he, Trumbull, and Barlow had composed the "performances";[19] and on January 20, 1787, after four numbers had been published, he wrote essentially the same news to Washington, adding that "Pointed ridicule is found to be of more efficacy than serious argumentation."[20] He wrote the verse portion of Number V and later included it in his *Miscellaneous Works*. Some have thought Lemuel Hopkins played the principal part in the series as a whole,[21] but it appears that his participation was limited to the last five numbers. In 1829 Samuel Knapp expressed the following wish: "The author of M'Fingal is still living, and could now, perhaps, tell us what share the different authors took in the Anarchiad. It is hoped that he will do it. Such an intimation would gratify the curious, and injure no one."[22] We must regret that Knapp's wish was not granted.

In this group known as the "Hartford Wits" Trumbull was the recognized leader. "The most conspicuous literary character of his day, in this country," according to S. G. Goodrich,[23] a brilliant conversationalist with extensive knowledge of polite letters, science, history, and politics, Trumbull shone in a circle which achieved a formidable reputation through Federalist propaganda and minor belletristic achievements. The group fluctuated in its unofficial membership with the passage of years, for some "wits" moved away and younger men joined the group. The names of the newer members usually mentioned are Rich-

ard Alsop, Theodore Dwight, Elihu Hubbard Smith, and Mason
Fitch Cogswell. In the mutually stimulating company of these
intelligent, literate, and influential men Trumbull must have
spent some of his happiest hours.

At times, Trumbull has been called a collaborator on the
Echo,[24] a political series of twenty numbers running from 1791
to 1805; but we now can say with reasonable certainty that this
opinion is in error. On February 9, 1793, Trumbull stated categorically to Jeremiah Wadsworth, "I never wrote in the *Echo*";[25]
and in a letter to John Adams on February 25 of the same year
he said, "I have never written in the *Echo*."[26] His illness in the
1790's and his abstention from political writing after he became
a judge in October 1801 make it unlikely that he contributed
any writing to the series after the date of the two letters mentioned. This conclusion is supported by Everest's statement in
1843, possibly based on firsthand information from Theodore
Dwight, that the poet never wrote for the *Echo*.[27]

Another work on which Trumbull collaborated was Barlow's
1785 book called *Doctor Watts's Imitation of the Psalms of David,
Corrected and Enlarged*,[28] one of the volumes representing the
transition from psalmody to hymnody. It has been thought that
"The exact authorship of the various revisions and even of the
completely new versions cannot be determined"[29] and that
Barlow wrote all the hymns,[30] but these opinions are no longer
valid. Trumbull's marked copy of the first edition tells a great
deal about the authorship of specific alterations and additions.
When the changes were minor, he simply placed an "x" beside
the passage affected; but when the psalm was what Barlow in
his preface called "considerably altered," Trumbull placed the
initial of the reviser beside it—for example, he placed a "T"
next to the common-metre version of Psalm XXI.

In the book we have examples of his verse which bring out
a facet of his character not often recognized. Because of his
potent and occasionally biting satire, few have perceived the
religious strain in his makeup; but it was there, as his son-in-law
Woodbridge and as his contributions to the new edition attest.

A comparison of Watts's version of stanzas three and four of
Psalm XXI with Trumbull's reveals how the latter excluded
references to the English monarchy:

Watts

Our King is the care of Heaven.

3　Then let the King on God alone
　　For timely Aid rely;
　　His Mercy shall support the Throne
　　And all our Wants supply.

4　But, righteous Lord, his stubborn Foes
　　Shall feel thy dreadful hand;
　　Thy vengeful Arm shall find out those
　　That hate his mild command.

Trumbull

National Blessings acknowledged.

3　In deep distress our injur'd land
　　Implor'd thy power to save;
　　For life we pray'd; thy bounteous hand
　　The timely blessing gave.

4　Thy mighty arm, eternal Power,
　　Oppos'd their deadly aim,
　　In mercy swept them from our shore,
　　And spread their sails with shame.

Perhaps unexpected from such a polemicist as Trumbull is verse which is less minatory than that of Watts, as in stanza four—indeed, in this and the other stanzas by the American the dominant idea is gratitude.

Of the twelve new psalms filling omissions by Watts, Trumbull composed four in whole or in part. According to his initialing, on Psalm XLIII he collaborated with Hopkins; and Psalm LII he wrote in a long-metre version and Hopkins in a common-metre. He also composed Psalm XXVIII and Psalm LXXIX, both of them in long metre. The latter reflects concern arising from the recently ended war. Trumbull's skill in versification, his competence in the four-stress line, his religious nature, and his patriotism combine in this psalm. Stanzas one and six read as follows:

Psalm LXXIX

For the distress of War.

1   BEHOLD, O GOD, what cruel foes,
     Thy peaceful heritage invade;
     Thy holy temple stands defil'd,
     In dust thy sacred walls are laid.
. . . .

6   So shall thy children, freed from death,
     Eternal songs of honour raise,
     And every future age shall tell,
     Thy sovereign power and pardoning grace.

The appeal to Providence was consistent with Trumbull's view that America was under God's protection. During the war, he stated that God designed "the deliverance of America";[31] in his revision of Psalm XXI, he expressed his belief that Providence aided the patriots; and years later he wrote, "It was the hand of heaven, that conducted the American Revolution, & provided & preserved the proper Instruments for our success."[32]

Of the hymns in the book, Trumbull initialed three as new, two by Barlow and one by himself. Though as a child Trumbull had feared he could not equal Watts, in Number LXVIII he handles the common metre as well as the Englishman did. The verse flows smoothly and the rhymes are accurate. In many respects, this hymn represents well the Trumbull who was not in controversy—it is orthodox, beneficent, pious, mellifluous, and reverent, as the following four of the six stanzas will attest:

Hymn LXVIII

A Hymn for Marriage

1   GREAT God, who form'd for social joys
     Our natures by thy power and grace,
     And join'd in blest connubial ties,
     The parents of our favour'd race.

2   Our Saviour, our ascended Lord,
     In Cana once a heavenly guest,
     Whose bounty cheer'd the friendly board
     Whose presence grac'd the nuptial feast.
. . . .

4 Let love assist their mutual toils,
  And every social bliss bestow;
  Increase each joy with friendly smiles,
  And share and soften every woe.

. . . .

6 When death dissolves these sacred ties,
  May each to happier realms remove;
  There meet and range the peaceful skies,
  In bands of everlasting love.

It was singularly fitting that the work on Watts's collection should have had Trumbull as one of its participants, for the Englishman was always one of the patriot's favorite authors. Indeed, Watts's *Horae Lyricae* was known to Trumbull in his early childhood, and it was the last volume in English which he read before his death in Detroit.[33]

In his collaboration after 1782, then, Trumbull's most important contributions were to Washington's "A Circular Letter . . . to the Governors of the several States," to Barlow's revision of Watts's psalms and hymns, and to *The Anarchiad*. His major work in Barlow's volume was identified by himself, but his portions in the other two were not. It seems indubitable, however, that his contributions to Washington's letter were distinguished by clarity and precision and those to *The Anarchiad* by piercing wit and clever verse.

II *Trumbull Alone*

Of the writing which Trumbull did alone during this period, most was prose, just as the greater proportion of his collaboration was verse. What poetry he did write individually was not polished or was merely penned for the new year. In his prose, on the other hand, he maintained a higher level. In it he demonstrated his continued skill in political satire, his emphasis on character, and his consistency as a patriot.

Trumbull's identified verse after 1782 is slight. The manuscript poem "——'s consolatory verses to his Master, on the loss of his small Clothes, in a Cytheraean Adventure" (1792), which sounds like a versified account of a local exploit, ends with a humorous reference to the French Revolution. ["The Bell of night struck one"], a stern rebuke to a profligate,[34] resembles "Characters" in the *Poetical Works;* but, since the untitled poem is dated May 1793, it was composed at least a decade later than the other. "Perfectability of Man" is a satiric treatment in iambic pentameter of Tom Paine, who had become the *bête noir* of the Federalists because of his outspoken egalitarianism.[35] Perhaps the best of the verse is found in the newsboy's "Address" to his patrons on New Year's Day in 1783, 1784, 1824, and 1825, all printed in Hartford and listed by Howard except for the last.[36]

The four poems, all in the octosyllabic couplet, are more good-humored than Hopkins's comparable "Guillotina" verses in the 1790's and more impersonal than Theodore Dwight's celebration of the new century on January 1, 1801. Trumbull provided an intelligent commentary on contemporary events for the readers, who rewarded the newsboy for the poem with a penny. The easy, conversational style, which occasionally included double rhymes, indicated how well the author had learned his lessons from Prior and Churchill.

The first two "addresses" reflect strongly Trumbull's major contemporary concerns. In 1783, the verses were reminiscent of *M'Fingal* in assuming toward the British the perky attitude of superiority from the opening line, "In England, where the poets scribble," to the ending gibes at the poet laureate Whitehead. Along the way, Trumbull called George III an "oaf" and celebrated "That freedom earn'd by foes repell'd." A year afterward, the war over and the army sent home, Trumbull praised the passage of copyright laws and concluded with a jocular wish for increased "Honesty and Understanding" on the part of the politicians and a love of freedom under the law by the people.

Forty years later Trumbull's verses contrast the strife in Europe with the peace at home. About politics he wrote,

> Democracy and Federalism,
> That caus'd such uproar once, and schism,
> Have stoutly fought their quarrel out,
> Till nought was left to fight about.

Once a strong partisan, he now could mellowly describe the old American political battles in verse which equaled that of the same type in the 1780's.

In 1825, Trumbull reviewed the world situation in the last

of these verses and found it improved; and, glancing toward home, he rejoiced in a recent defeat of the caucus in New York. After finishing the first draft of the "address," he augmented by fourteen lines the section praising Lafayette, who in 1824 had been honored in Hartford with a breakfast at which Trumbull was a guest. Characteristically, the poet included a section on freedom:

> Yet Freedom sees her right protected,
> Where'er her standard is erected.
> The Turkish moons are in eclipse,
> The Greeks, as usual, burn their ships;
> On Andes' heights, her laurels wave
> In triumph o'er Iturbide's grave;
> In scorn of Gallia's slavish chains,
> Bold Hayti still her state maintains,
> Where king Christophe to scape his doom,
> By suicide obtained a tomb.

Such are his known newsboy's verses—the fluently expressed commentary and sentiments of an astute patriotic observer who championed freedom.

Trumbull's reputation as a political propagandist has rested upon *M'Fingal* and his undetermined contributions to *The Anarchiad,* but it seems likely that it should be based also on a substantial amount of anonymous prose about government and politics. According to an account written a few years after his death, "Volumes would hardly contain the newspaper and pamphlet publications, of which he was the author; but they were all anonymous, and put out most generally through the printing presses of states other than his own."[37] The earlier political prose has not yet been certainly identified, but some of the later has. In it, Trumbull steadily devoted his pen to the welfare of his country as he saw it.[38] He advocated the establishment of a firmer national government under the Constitution, he defended Washington's policy of neutrality between France and England, and, last, he consistently opposed caucuses as inimical to democracy.

Occasionally he candidly described his own political writings. On February 5, 1791, in a letter to John Adams he asserted that he had censured persons as well as measures with a freedom most citizens would not have attempted. He enjoyed his independence, but he occasionally regretted somewhat the potency of satire as a weapon in political battles, as he confessed to Adams in 1793:

Shall I own to You, that when I could divest myself of the vanity of an Author, & consider myself only as one of the human race, & *so* liable to my average of general degradation in the scale of Beings, I have been mortified & ashamed at the success of some of my own satirical productions, as well as those written by others. I have often seen that a well-timed stroke of humour against a measure proposed, or a lucky burlesque nickname fixed on an influential man, have had more effect in destroying the influence of the Man, or preventing the success of the measure, than if all the reason ever bestowed on mankind had been distilled in an alembic into Alchohol [*sic*], & given in proper doses to the Legislature, or the People.[39]

Most of the time, though, he saw himself as an unshackled citizen who spoke candidly on all questions because of his concern for the nation and who castigated those who "deserted their principles."[40] He believed, furthermore, he had been "as useful in public affairs in this way" as he could have been in any office.

In "The American," a series of seven political essays published in the Connecticut *Courant*,[41] Trumbull convincingly demonstrated his ability to sustain a series of articles on contemporary affairs. He produced informational, persuasive, and ironically satirical essays championing the Federalist viewpoint. Always lucid, he made astute observations on the French Revolution, titles for government officials, leveling tendencies, and other topics. If he had had good health, he might have written an even better set of articles in his crisp, controlled prose.

Trumbull himself is the authority for ascribing the series to him. On February 9, 1793, after five of the essays had been printed, he claimed them as his in a letter to Jeremiah Wadsworth: "*The American* is wholly & avowedly mine. It appeared to me that the People wanted some direct Information on the subjects I have handled." On February 25, he expressed substantially the same idea in a letter to John Adams; and he added, "I have reason to believe the Essays have made some impression." Adams responded that "The American," as well as the "Echo," had been both popular and effective in Massachusetts, and he left money for subscribing to both Hartford papers.[42]

Since the aim in "The American" is informational as well as polemic, the French Revolution is treated dispassionately in the first essay. It opened with the assertion that "All great revolutions are effected more by the influence of the passions, than of reason,"[43] and it explained the excesses which had occurred in the great upheaval. It ended on a hopeful note: "May her government soon be settled on the firm foundation of equal liberty, and may the period of distress and anarchy be so shortened, that it may not serve to deter other nations from following the glorious example of opposing the claims of tyranny, and vindicating from despotism the just rights of man." Obviously Trumbull took a rather favorable view of the French Revolution in its early days.

Though the first number was nonpartisan in tone, the second was quite frankly Federalistic, as the vigorous opening made clear: "When we observe the beneficial effects of moral and religious principles among the people of the United States, and the happiness we have enjoyed under the new constitution of our government, it seems astonishing that any person should wish to exchange these advantages for the modern refinements of Sceptics and Levellers—and still more strange, that such a person should be supported by a powerful party, and assisted by the influence of many characters, otherwise truly respectable."[44] The remainder of the short essay condemned Paine and censured Jefferson for supporting him.

The third and fourth numbers distinguished between honorary titles and hereditary succession,[45] a distinction of aid to John Adams, who had been accused of holding monarchical principles. With the clarity and forcefulness Trumbull had employed earlier in "The Correspondent" he established his case by pointing out the necessity for some appellations for the top governmental officials and by identifying as harmful only those terms which conferred privilege or inherited rank. Opposing the contemporary French usage of *"Citizen,"* he contended that that term itself was not egalitarian because it set the citizen off from the disfranchised rabble. He saw no danger from existing governmental titles in America and lamented demagogic warnings about them by newspaper editors.

The fifth number was devoted to some of the more important controversial questions about government.[46] The opponents of the Federalists could not argue with most of the answers, but the reply to the first question, *"Are all mankind equal?"* must have nettled them. Trumbull wrote, "I answer, yes, in all their rights of personal liberty, consistent with just laws, and of protection in the enjoyment of their private property. I add that all have equal claim to their proportionate influence in the appointment of public rulers." This Federalist emphasis upon "their proportionate influence" could hardly have pleased the people of small wealth.

The sixth essay, a long one, castigated the anti-Federalists.[47] After demonstrating the need for the Constitution, Trumbull pointed out that the political opposition had attacked the President and all his supporters and that it had tested its power in the election of the Vice-President. Trumbull thoroughly analyzed the election, which his friend Adams won, and then asserted that the opposition had a new group of Irish political writers who fancied that they knew better what was good for the country than the natives themselves. The reference here was to the Careys (Mathew, John, and James), who were supporters of Jefferson.

When Trumbull completed the series on April 15 with the seventh essay, he returned to his favorite device of irony in a letter, purportedly from "Aristides," that berated the "levellers."[48] The reputed letter writer says, for example, that Washington has twice been elected President unanimously despite the fact that he himself had more right to the high office because he had such little influence that the people's rights would not be endangered. And in a later paragraph Trumbull satirized the egalitarians by reflecting that the French had produced in the guillotine the perfect leveling or equalizing "method"—"It is to behead the man...." With this potent stroke he ended the series.

In Trumbull's correspondence lies the story behind another of his contributions in the bitter political warfare in the early years under the Constitution. In a letter from Philadelphia on January 31, 1793, came an account to Trumbull from his friend John Adams about "The natural History of *Mother Carey's Chickens.*"[49] After explaining the fright the birds inspire, Adams made his application to the three Careys. He belittled the three Irish immigrants as "Fugitives from Justice" who hovered around the "federal Ship," and he complained that they constantly stayed near Jefferson, James Madison, and John Beckley, the Clerk of the House of Representatives. Trumbull utilized this political information not only in the sixth essay of "The American" but also in a separate and more extended newspaper article. On April 27, 1793, he wrote to Adams that if the latter had seen John Fenno's *Gazette of the United States* he might have noticed a story which had been reprinted by a number of newspapers.

Trumbull's adaptation for propaganda of the news from Adams appeared in the *Gazette of the United States* on April 13, 1793.[50] For Trumbull, quoting a bogus letter to make a point was a familiar device, as he had used it both in "The Correspondent" and in "The American"; and he had participated in the spurious correspondence preceding *The Anarchiad*. Now, in the letter on Mother Carey's chickens, he proved how he could develop into political propaganda a resemblance someone else first saw between some birds and the anti-Federalist group represented by the Careys and Freneau.

After explaining the nature of Mother Carey's chickens and stating "that a certain great modern philosopher and politician, has lately got a small brood of them into his possession," he gave a pretended "extract" of a letter from "the Latitude of Philadelphia." For it he borrowed from Adams the "federal ship," Mother Carey's chickens, and the Virginians; and he combined them with the *Aeneid* into an imaginary account of a landing by the birds on a ship at sea. They were made to sound like jackasses, to shout leveling slogans, to speak with an Irish brogue, and to mouth anti-Federalist propaganda. Then followed their departure:

At length, at a given signal, they all rose on the wing, and went off singing Lillibullero in concert, leaving behind, like the harpies, a most terrible stench, and our decks all covered with their ordure. We have ever since had dangerous weather, and there is every appearance of a storm from the south. We trust, however, to be able to weather the squall, and so God send the good ship to her destined port.

Your's, etc.

The publisher of the foregoing letter adds, that in his opinion, these ill-boding Chickens are the same creatures as the Grecian Harpies, whom they resemble completely in manners, habits, and the prophetic spirit. In proof of which he refers us to Virgil's description of them, in the 3rd book of the Eneid [*sic*].

It should be noted that the inclusion of "Lillibullero" as a song is a gibe at Irish Catholics.

A political pamphlet which appeared after the poet and his friends were turned out of their judgeships in 1819 is *The Mischiefs of Legislative Caucuses, Exposed in an Address to the people of Connecticut*. Although on its title page authorship is ascribed to "Trumbull," neither Cowie nor Howard attributes it to him; Richard Purcell, however, does so without reservation.[51] The pamphlet sounds as though it were written not by the poet but by someone who knew him and his political beliefs very well, for the ideas plainly are ones which he strongly supported. His opposition to political caucuses in 1819 would be consistent with his earlier position on them, as is evident from a number of his statements, particularly those in a letter to John Adams on July 21, 1805 (misdated 1801).

Two nonpolitical works further illustrate Trumbull's sustained skill in prose. The first, the *Biographical Sketch of the Character of Governor Trumbull*, was published in Hartford in 1809 upon the death of the state's chief officer. The word *character* in its title is significant for revealing much about the subject and about the author himself. A second cousin of the deceased governor, the poet briefly traced the family tree; gracefully paid tribute to the dead man's father, the Revolutionary War governor; and then dwelt on the character traits which had won the respect and esteem of everyone, no matter what his political affiliation might be. In his eulogy, just as in his memorial for St. John in 1771, Trumbull avoided bombast and made a sincere tribute to the former governor and to integrity in high office in sentences such as the following: "But the strength of judgment and an enlightened understanding, the steady exertions of friendship and patriotism, and the virtues of a heart, regulating all its conduct by the principles of justice, morality and religion, can alone form the man of true greatness of character, and value in society."[52] Although the brief biography was published anonymously, it was written by the poet, for he identified it in his own handwriting as his.[53]

The second nonpolitical essay of these years was written in 1826, the year in which Trumbull responded to a request for a Fourth-of-July address with an able composition delivered for him by A. G. Whitney. Appropriately on this fiftieth anniversary of the Declaration of Independence some main points stressed by the venerable judge were "the enlightened spirit of genuine Liberty,"[54] the Constitution, and the eminent men to whom God had given the responsibility of the American cause. Taken as a whole, the address contained the ordered prose which its author had exhibited for decades, but the hortatory ending was something new: "Let us then rejoice, in contemplation of our present felicity, and in view of our future prospects. Let us enjoy with gratitude the rich bounties of heaven. With patriotic ardor & fraternal affection, let us join with our brethren throughout the Union, in celebrating this joyful anniversary, the birthday of our rising Empire—the day on which commenced the splendid Era of American Independence, Freedom and Glory." Gone were all rancor, partisanship, and satire in the emphasis on patriots and patriotism. Unknown to Trumbull at the time was the fact that two of the men whom he praised, John Adams and Thomas Jefferson, died on the very day his speech was delivered.

Though Trumbull's literary production was sharply curtailed after he completed *M'Fingal,* it did not cease entirely. In the collaborations, his wit, his patriotism, his knowledge of belles lettres, and his religious cast of mind are apparent. His known verse other than the psalms and hymn he wrote for Barlow is less skillful and less forceful than the earlier, and it served mainly to help the newsboys gather New Year's pennies. His political prose, staunchly Federalist, is cogent, learned and witty—considerably above the level of most political propaganda. And his other prose, strong and supple, tells much about its author in its stress on two lifelong interests: character and freedom.

"The Minutiae of Criticism"

ALTHOUGH Trumbull has been known almost exclusively as a satirical poet, his extant literary criticism should be included in any evaluation of him as a man of letters. Cowie, who believed that under more favorable circumstances Trumbull probably would have revised and published some writings left in manuscript,[1] stated that the Tyler Papers at Cornell University "contain materials of real importance to the student of early American criticism."[2] Those manuscripts and other sources give us an incomplete record, but they contain enough of the poet's critical views to warrant an examination.

The main sources for Trumbull's literary opinions and evaluations are the Tyler Papers at Cornell and the William Woodbridge Papers at the Detroit Public Library. Additional sources of information are the poet's correspondence found at other locations, articles in periodicals, and a letter by William Moseley Holland,[3] who appears to be the only person who has left a record of the remarks on literature which Trumbull made in conversation.[4] Except for this letter, the sources mentioned were written by the poet for his own studious enjoyment; for advice, encouragement, and support of others; and for the defense of his friend Humphreys, a task accomplished in three published pieces of literary criticism.

Trumbull's impressive qualifications for evaluating belles lettres included temperament, general knowledge, and a high degree of literacy. About the first of these, he late in life remarked that it was unusual "that any one, tho' formed with the keenest sensibility, & the most extravagantly romantic feelings, should have an innate attention to the minutiae of Criticism."[5] And few persons were as knowledgeable, for he was an omnivorous reader, not only as a child but also as an adult. He even damaged his health by excessive reading during the Revolutionary War because he was "determined to be the most learned Man in America,"[6] as he wrote to Adams. Though he did not reach primacy as a "learned Man," he certainly was one of the most literate persons of his time.

His acquaintance with good reading was encouraged by a favorable intellectual milieu all his life. At home his parents gave him an early start; and at college he had the fortunate company of Joseph Howe, Nathan Strong, Timothy Dwight, Joel Barlow, and David Humphreys in scholarly discussions. To this bright coterie must be added Silas Deane, friend and mentor. In Hartford, Trumbull was surrounded by a congenial group of outstanding men, some of them members of the "Friendly Club" to which he referred in the "Memoir." These persons, under his guidance as their erudite and witty leader, engaged in stimulating conversations about men and letters. All these factors contributed to the extensive learning apparent in his numerous references to Classical, Italian, Spanish, French, and English writers, many of whose works he included in his library.

Trumbull's literary criteria and topics on which he expressed opinions were fairly common in his day, but his application of the standards and his style of writing were individual. The standards were, first, neo-Classicism, derived especially from Horace, Addison, and Pope; second, common sense, probably owing much to Kames; and third, morality, likely stemming from his home environment and his reading of Watts. These were applied with independence, honesty, and candor in a style which was all the more fresh and vigorous because of the freedom inherent in notebook writing and letters and, in one instance, because of the warmth generated by a fatuous review of his friend Humphreys's work.

I Critical Persuasions

Trumbull's ideas on critics and criticism, language, description, originality, and the novel as a genre are typical of his character and his educational background. Writing about critics and criticism, he condemned evaluations with which he disagreed, he differed with such favorites of his as Lord Kames, and he showed preference for a satirical type of literary criticism. He was irritated by what he considered inadequacy in many critics of his day and throughout his work scoffed at their opinions about contemporary writing. In a letter to Silas Deane of October 20, 1775, for example, he derided the "merely grammatical critics"; and to Elkanah Watson he gave the advice that some small mistakes might be left " 'as they are, for the small critics to nibble upon; for as they are the proper domesticks in the literary family, it is but just that their masters should give them some crumbs for their subsistence.' "[7] He also lamented the dictatorial tendency of some English critics to "direct their readers when to laugh or cry, be pleased or displeased according to the exactest rules of criticism";[8] and he complained about what he considered unreasoned British contempt for American writing.[9]

Believing that ignorance and a lack of perceptiveness are found in some opinions about literature, Trumbull wrote three essays condemning these faults and illustrating the vitiating effect they could have on interpretations of belles lettres. In August 1781 he exclaimed, "How ignorant do most of the Modern Critics appear to be of the true Character of those antient Writers, of whom they affect to speak with the utmost familiarity!"[10] To prove his point, he asserted that Cicero had been "held forth, as a pattern of Selfconceit, & the most vainglorious of all antient Writers," but that an examination of statements by Isocrates, Horace, Ovid, and Pliny would show that boasting was characteristic of their day. In another sketch, "On a Passage in L. Kaims," he disproved the Scotchman's contention that in Pope's *Eloisa to Abelard* some ideas were appropriate to its author but not to the heroine. And, in the short essay "Socrates," he charged critics with repeating the errors of others when they asserted that the philosopher acted from a sense of duty in asking that a cock be sacrificed to Aesculapius. The truth, Trumbull said, was that Socrates lived up to his name the "Ironist" by requesting the sacrifice, an action meaning that his enemies unwittingly were sending him to eternal health in the Elysian Fields.

Given Trumbull's bent for mimicry and satire, it is only natural that in an unpolished and unpublished essay on critics he focused his remarks on the satirical type.[11] He first divided the critics into three classes: (1) Aristotle and others who seek by metaphysical discussion to arrive at precepts upon which "they form dogmatical maxims & endeavor to establish a Code of critical laws (& system)"; (2) Longinus and others, "men of delicate feelings, just discernment & elegant taste," who "point [out] the beauties & defects of authors"; and (3) "Satirical Critics," and with this group he is concerned.

As Trumbull sees such critics, they utilize a method consisting "in the exhibition & exposure of all the faults in style, manner, taste & sentiment of Authors selected as the objects of ridicule, & in an accurate imitation of their worst modes of composition." According to him, there were some examples of this type of criticism among the ancients but many more among recent writers. The modern popularity of the method was important, he thought, because "this kind of exposure has been found the most effectual for correct'g the public taste," which at the time, he said, admired "every thing that is novel, & extravagant and opposed to just principles, & common sense & pure morals." These modern authors took their lead, he believed, from Isaac Hawkins Browne, who in *The Pipe of Tobacco* set an eighteenth-century standard for this mimicking criticism. Works of the kind Trumbull mentioned with approval were *The Rehearsal*, by the Duke of Buckingham; *The Dunciad*, by Pope; *The Baviad* and *The Maeviad*, by William Gifford; *Warreniana; The Anti-Jacobin*; and *Rejected Addresses*.

The quotations in the preceding paragraph come from the 1820's, when Trumbull showed greatest interest in satirical criticism as a valid literary type; but it should be noted that, contrary to one opinion,[12] he had recognized its potential over half a century earlier and was intrigued by it. In "Critical Reflections" he commended Browne's effective mimicking of the distinctive styles of six different poets. Among them was Swift, the imitation of whom Trumbull called "the severest Satire ever written against him & what even Swift must have been unable to answer." And as early as 1769, whether Trumbull knew Browne's critical work at that time or not, he himself exposed the excesses of James Hervey's *Meditations and Contemplations* (1746) by mimicking the work in the seventh number of "The Meddler":

. . . they dressed for advantage and not for ornament. Necessity was their instructor, and plainness their model. Where were the periwigs loading the shoulders, and themselves loaded with mealy honours; those stupendous amphitheatres, amidst whose vast expansive rounds, heads unnumbered move, and to our limited sight, heads unnumbered are lost? where was the sack, that behind, with long, long excursion, sweeps the affrighted earth with its enormous train? where the coat beaming with golden radiance, where the petticoat extending its ample round? where those variegated decorations, that bestow on the wearer, such a striking resemblance to the butterfly expanding his gilded wings, or a cloud tinged with the bright radiances of setting Phoebus.[13]

Then, busy with his law practice, his judicial duties, and his family, he apparently abandoned the congenial satirical literary criticism for many years; and he returned to writing about it only when he had the enforced leisure of an unwillingly retired judge.

A strong point in Trumbull's qualifications as a literary critic was his continued interest in some aspects of language and usage. All his life he supported simplicity, accuracy, and vigor, qualities which he found best exemplified in Elizabethan English.[14] It is apparent from his writings and from the statements of others that he observed linguistic changes carefully, as, for example, a contemporary shift in usage involving *vocation* and *avocation,* a phenomenon he disapproved of as unnecessary and unsound.[15] At age nineteen he objected to the contemporary popularity of periphrasis, by which a man was not called a hog but rather "that animal, before which we are commanded not to throw pearls";[16] and in later years he repeatedly condemned Samuel Johnson's language as encouragement to pedanticism in English.

Much intrigued by etymology, he commented on changes from Latin to Italian as being primarily in the spelling, such as "*major,* Latin becomes *maggiore* in Italian"; and he observed that although numerous words were evidently of Asiatic origin they had not been traced through their intermediate steps from the Oriental languages to English. When he copied into his notebooks many expressions used by Dugald Stewart, the Scottish philosopher, he carefully mentioned any new sense employed.[17] In marginalia on his copy of Noah Webster's *A Collection of*

Essays and Fugitiv Writings, he questioned the lexicographer's statements on the origin of the Greek word *Theos,* the idea that *"dom bec"* meant *"liber judicum,"* and the contention that *"Parochia* cannot be the origin of parish; for it waz not a Roman word."[18] When Webster called Samuel Johnson "a good Latin and Greek scholar," Trumbull jotted tersely, "A tolerable Latin scholar, & no more."[19] Later, after leaving the bench, he used his knowledge of language and languages to good advantage by examining "a considerable portion" of the manuscript of Webster's dictionary of 1828.[20]

Most of Trumbull's ideas on poetry are to be found in scattered comments, but some were set down with more system in "A Critical Dissertation on descriptive Poetry," the fifth number of the "Speculative Essays." For it, he derived some of his views from Kames and possibly some from Hugh Blair. When Trumbull wrote that the mind is more affected by the concrete than by the abstract, he may have reflected some comments by Kames in the twenty-first chapter of *Elements of Criticism;*[21] and, when he maintained that poets who have excelled in pictorial power have always been accorded the first rank, he probably had Blair's ideas in mind.[22] He openly acknowledged his debt to Kames when he attributed to the Scotchman the concept that whether description was generalized or particularized, it should "raise an ideal presence of the object."[23] He seems to have departed from Kames and developed his own ideas when he continued his discussion. According to "the rules of Nature and Homer," he said, when objects are pictured as seen from a distance, the description should be general; when from nearby, as in the midst of a battle, it should be particular. Details should be selected according to the style of a poem, the choices being ones for which rules cannot possibly be given. In the arrangement of details, an author should follow "nature." For a complete picture, when one is needed, the poet should first tell what he intends to portray, and then present an overall view. As a model of pictorial strength, Trumbull cited a passage by Thomas Parnell depicting an angel. During his entire adult life he maintained these opinions, and on the basis of them he told William Moseley Holland in 1825 that Homer had descriptive skill but Virgil lacked it.[24]

"Critical Reflections" contains Trumbull's ideas on originality, a topic discussed in English books such as Richard Hurd's *Dissertation on Poetical Imitation* (1751) and *On the Marks of Imitation* (1757). It may be, of course, that he had not read Hurd but had been stimulated to writing, in his notebook, about originality because of other discussions concerning the topic since he made a distinciton between two types of originality: "manner," which meant "method, style, expression, versification etc."; and "thought," which Hurd did not make. When Trumbull assessed seriatim the works of Pope, Swift, Butler, Prior, Churchill, Edward Young, Gay, Steele, Addison, Thomson, Gray, William Shenstone, Goldsmith, James Beattie, Johnson, Thomas Moore, Henry Brooke, William Mason, and Browne, more authors are adjudged original in style than in thought, among them being Pope, Thomson, Johnson, Gray, Shenstone, and Goldsmith. Calling Goldsmith's *The Deserted Village* a "masterpiece," Trumbull praised what he termed the "little circumstances" accentuating the beauty in its descriptions; and he commended Goldsmith, Gray, and Shenstone for simplicity.

An example of Trumbull's own style and of his remarks in this notebook essay is that concerning Swift: "In what then is Swift an original? In his humorous descriptions. He is a poetical painter of caricaturas; a Hogarth among writers. In this he is original & unrivalled. He sets every description before the eye in the strongest and most lively colours, & omits none of the minutiae of Ridicule. In other respects his friend Arbuthnot & his Successor Sterne, tho' by no means his equals in fine writing, are much more of Originals than he." Among other comments about Swift is that the chief virtue of his style lay in "correctness" and suitability to the subject. Swift and the other men named are regarded as less original than the anonymous author of an elegy on William Pitt at the time he was made a peer. This poem is praised for "boldness" in the "figures," newness of versification, and an unprecedented combination of "Sublime & Pathetic Satire"—qualities making it the most original poem in fifty years. Unsystematic though these "reflections" are, they contain so many keen insights that we could wish Trumbull had developed them into a rounded essay.

Although we might expect Trumbull as a neo-Classicist to react negatively to the novel as a relatively new literary form,[25] he did not object to the genre as such but rather to improbability, to exaggerated descriptions,[26] and to the moral content of some novels. In one of his essays, "On Romances and Novels,"[27] he contended that authors were driven "to have recourse to extraordinary Accidents, or improbable bravery" by the fact that, since Cervantes, they had had to satisfy the public's thirst for the marvelous without the aid of giants and other figures from the old romances. Partially excusing the novelists, he said it was unfair to demand the marvelous from them and then deprive them of a reasonable means to satisfy the public appetite. He cited Richardson's *Sir Charles Grandison* and Henry Fielding's *Tom Jones* as examples of the "improbable meetings, impossible bravery, & unaccountable accidents [which] make up the whole circle of the modern Novellist's invention." To buttress his case, he cited Goldsmith's *The Vicar of Wakefield* and Brooke's *The Fool of Quality* as further proof. In questioning the moral content of certain novels, he referred disparagingly to Sterne's *Tristram Shandy* and, in the last essay of "The Meddler," he objected to Richardson's Lovelace.

Rather than frowning upon the novel as such, Trumbull in fact gave a number of indications that he approved of it. In "Critical Reflections" (1778), he not only made no strictures on it but praised Richardson for incorporating revealing details of everyday life and for understanding female psychology. Richardson and Jean François Marmontel, he observed, were the only "two writers who appear to have perfectly understood the Fair Sex." Furthermore, he himself made an attempt at the genre in "The Mathematical Metaphysician," of which unfortunately only four chapters survive; for Trumbull's was one of the earliest trials at novel writing in America. Also, he wrote on January 8, 1772, to Silas Deane that, if his ideas on a project against sceptics and Deists grew, he might "plan a work on the Subject," among the possibilities being "an allegory or novel." He probably began reading fiction early in life, for he wrote in 1773 that he had taken "leave of novels & romances"[28] as he departed for Boston to study law. Later he commended parts of James Fenimore Cooper's *Lionel Lincoln*,[29] and he included in his own library novels such as *Don Quixote* (both in Spanish and in French) and Benjamin Disraeli's *Vivian Grey*.

II *Literary Appraisals*

Many of Trumbull's critical ideas are contained in his statements about particular books on which he was giving advice or
which he had read. To nonfiction volumes, he applied common
sense and a moral standard. We do not have his comments on
the Reverend Benjamin Trumbull's *A General History of the
United States of America,* the first volume of which the poet
and Dwight critically examined in manuscript,[30] but we have
letters revealing his advice to some authors.

Despite the fact that Trumbull himself always wrote according
to a high standard, he recognized that some books must suit a
popular audience and the subject. Concerning a geography book,
for example, he counseled the Reverend Jedidiah Morse that
volumes written for a mass audience should aim at intelligibility
and should avoid the pedantic.[31] Accordingly, he urged that
words such as *"immigrating"* and *"percolating"* be dropped. For
a travel book he urged Elkanah Watson to use "an easy, lively,
familiar style"[32] rather than "the laborious stiffness and pedantry
of Johnson, or the florid elegance of Gibbon." Anyone writing
for general consumption, Trumbull said, should seek to be understood by his readers rather than to be praised by those who are
scholars. Not given to formalism despite his vast learning,
Trumbull used his common sense when he gave practical suggestions to men such as Watson, who submitted his books to
Trumbull while they were still in manuscript.[33]

Applying a moral standard to books, Trumbull occasionally
was irritated by what he considered the meretricious titillations
of spicy travelogues. Anent volumes by Francis Le Vaillant[34]
and Mauritius Benyowsky,[35] for instance, he acidly wrote, "It is
a pity we have no journal of *Travels to Botany Bay.* The Amours
of the Convicts with the Nymphs of *New South Wales* are a
desideratum in English Literature. Perhaps it might be hoped
for from the pen of the celebrated *Barrington,* should he meet
with due encouragement from the Mecaenas [*sic*] of Sidney
Cove."[36] He had, however, no objection to travel books as
such—in fact, he owned volumes of the type by many authors,
such as Thomas McKenney, Henry Schoolcraft, George Keppel,
Daines Barrington, Thomas Jefferson Hogg, and Henry E.
Dwight.

When assessing the prose style of some of his contemporaries, Trumbull found they fell short of the best eighteenth-century standards. At a time when Franklin was idolized at home and abroad, Trumbull wrote that the popular statesman and philosopher "never rose to high eminence as a literary character."[37] He judged that Paine excelled in "vivacity of imagination and strength of expression, in force as well as sophistry of argument,"[38] but that *Common Sense,* valuable as it was for its time, deservedly aroused smiles later for "its ignorance and extravagance." Evaluating Edmund Burke's *Philippic on the Revolution in France,* Trumbull wrote to his close friend Adams with the freedom permissible in a private letter:

As a philippic, it undoubtedly contains many highly laboured passages, expressed in forcible & pompous language, abounding in brilliant allusion, & full of satirical wit, indignation & contempt. But where is the sublimity and pathos, tho' often attempted, which can establish him as the rival of Cicero or Demosthenes? He has written on the Sublime and Beautiful—he affects to be a sublime & beautiful Writer—but he mistakes the bent of his Genius. His predominant talent is Wit—a sprightliness of allusion & brilliance of metaphor, well calculated to figure in the productions of a Swift or a Butler, but which loses its principal grace when tortured into sublimity, & obscured by the affected rotundity of pompous period.

Examine a sample.

"The *anodyne draught* of oblivion, thus drugged, is well calculated to preserve a *galling wakefulness,* & to feed the *living ulcer* of a *corroding memory.* Thus to administer the *opiate potion* of amnesty, *powdered* with all the *ingredients of scorn & contempt,* is to hold to his lips, instead of the *balm of hurt minds,* the *cup of human misery* full to the brim, & to force him to *drink it to the dregs.*"

Is this Style? is it sense? is it English?[39]

Scanty though these critical remarks are, they nevertheless indicate the sensitivity of their author to prose style.

Had Trumbull's papers been preserved in their entirety, or had Dr. Cogswell and others passed on his remarks, we should be able to make a more accurate appraisal of the poet's dramatic criticism. As it is, we must depend on the correspondence with James Abraham Hillhouse, an aspiring young dramatist, who repeatedly turned to the judge for advice.[40] From the materials available, it seems safe to conclude that Trumbull respected the Greek dramatists, the Elizabethans, and the Jacobeans most, and that he venerated Shakespeare as "the matchless genius of the drama; endowed with the most noble extravagance of imagination, the strongest powers of humour, the sovereign command of the passions, and the keenest inspection into all the mazes of the human soul."[41]

Trumbull's comments to Hillhouse contain most of his views on blank verse, a form to which he was not opposed and which he had attempted in the first draft of his elegy on Buckingham St. John.[42] Warning Hillhouse that it could be prolix, he said, "Single thoughts are drawn out, like threads in a glass work to immense length, wonderful for their tenuity, glittering tho' unsubstantial. The style in blank verse ought to be as much condensed as that of Pope. Every elliptical form of expression, every omission of the relative or connective, that does not lead to harshness or obscurity tends to give strength as well as conciseness."[43] Notwithstanding that Trumbull in this passage strongly urged concision in blank verse, he was aware as early as 1784 that the freedom permitted in the form posed little danger to the versification.[44] There was a special difficulty in plays, though, because at the very time dramatic poetry "should indeed resemble prose as far as is consistent with melody & correctness of versification,"[45] the blank verse should not become too much like prose or lapse into it.

For *Percy's Masque* (1819) he gave Hillhouse suggestions which showed insight and which emphasized honesty and vigor. He thought the character of Rook should be "a little heightened"[46] because a villain should "be either daring or artful" and Percy should show "more magnanimity." Cant expressions such as *"Gramercy"* borrowed from Shakespeare should be omitted because they "are only vulgar abbreviations" and often not understood. He told his dislike of alexandrines and "the turgid, declamatory style" in blank verse. He advised Hillhouse that condensation would strengthen the style and that the verse bore more resemblance to the listless lines of Nicholas Rowe and Addison than to the vigorous ones of Shakespeare. To make his point, he cited an ancient authority: *"Obstat,* says Quintilian, *quicquid non adjuvat."* He praised the play as better "in its plot & execution" than any tragedy written in England for fifty years, and he added that the compliment was small because English drama had been rather unproductive during that period. He aligned himself with the Elizabethans and Jacobeans in a passage advising Hillhouse that in any future, more emotional drama the playwright should "adopt a stile more concise & abrupt, figures more daring, sudden transitions, & all the vehemence of the early English dramatists," who composed their plays before a sickly and affected French taste had prevailed and had overcome the British simplicity.

On April 4, 1820, Trumbull wrote to Hillhouse about *Percy's Masque* and asked if he wanted published a brief review which would compare the drama with Classical and modern plays. Apparently Hillhouse answered that he did, for the June 1820 *New-York Literary Journal, and Belles-Lettres Repository* carried such a review in the form of a letter from Trumbull to C. S. Van Winkle, the editor. This comparison, in the introductory passage, summarizes Trumbull's opinions concerning the trends in drama and reinforces some points made in his letter two years earlier:

False taste, erroneous criticism, and mistaken ideas of the nature of dramatic poetry, have almost ruined the spirit of the English stage. Its declension is owned and lamented by their most judicious and distinguished critics. Pompous declamation, and labored descriptions, more in the epic than tragic style, have been too often substituted for the language of nature and the passions. From the aera of Shakespeare to the suppression of plays in the time of Cromwell, the British theatre, amidst all its imperfections, maintained its own natural and original character. But on its revival in the reign of Charles II, the serious Drama was degraded by a servile imitation of the laboured pomp of the French rhyming tragedy; and its vigor cramped by submission to the arbitrary rules of the modern school of criticism. The ease and graceful simplicity of the dialogue were exchanged for bombastic language, and artificial sentiment. The actors were introduced to declaim at each other in set heroic speeches, and the writers of plays ceased to be natural by striving to become poetical.

In the main portion of the laudatory review, he praised *Percy's Masque* for "examples of sublime and pathetic sentiments and descriptions," satisfactory plot, skillful dialogue, suitable diction, and excellent versification.

Five years later he gave more of his opinions on drama when

writing to Hillhouse about *Hadad* (which not only he but also
William Cullen Bryant was reading to suggest improvements).
Characterizing Henry Hart Milman's style, he said that "[It]
is so flat & prosaic, that I could almost imagine I was reading
Southy's [*sic*] odes & pilgrimage to Waterloo."[47] In another
striking observation he wrote, "The *Devil in love* forms the
principal machinery of the poets of the day, & supplies the place
of all the Gods & Goddesses of the old mythology." Practicing
playwrights might have given Hillhouse more advice on details;
but few, if any, could have couched their ideas in more colorful
prose. Grateful for the suggestions so vividly expressed, Hillhouse
dedicated to Trumbull the second volume of *Dramas, Discourses,
and Other Pieces.*[48]

Fortunately, Trumbull left a fairly large record of his ideas
on poets and poetry in his published work, in his manuscripts,
in his letters, and in his conversations with friends. From these
sources, it is evident that he measured poetry by such criteria
as control, organization, conciseness, simplicity, sublimity, vigor,
and descriptive power. Behind his judgments lay his familiarity
with the past and with his present, from Homer into the nine-
teenth century. Scholarly and candid, he stated his evaluations
with lucidity and precision. Later generations have concurred
in many of Trumbull's opinions about poetry even though they
have departed from his emphasis on morals and on Classical
control. Not only is it useful for us to have his views on the
larger topics and on the minutiae, but it is fitting that a man
himself known for his verse should have had them preserved.

Thoroughly acquainted with Classical literature, Trumbull left
references to Greek and Roman writers scattered throughout his
work. He apparently enjoyed the Greek dramatists, but above
them all he placed Homer, master of "sublimity."[49] Of the Roman
poets, he referred to Juvenal, Horace, Persius, Ovid, and Virgil.
He praised Ovid as the only Roman poet who "was master of
the liquid softness of the Latin language";[50] and, concerning
Virgil, he noted an emphasis upon words containing the letter
m,[51] meritorius "judgment,"[52] "elegance & correctness,"[53] and an
aiming at "pomp of sound & force of expression."[54] Apparently
he cherished the work of the Roman poets, as he memorized
much of their work and could quote copiously from them, especially from Horace, his favorite.[55]

He alluded to many poets of continental Europe, as, for instance, to Tasso, whose "luxuriant imagination" he mentioned;[56] but it was to the British poets that he referred most often. Taken as a whole, his writings indicate familiarity with William Langland, Edward Fairfax, Butler, Rochester, Buckingham, John Dryden, and a number of others to whom he alluded occasionally. Acquainted with Spenser's "Epithalamion" and *Faerie Queene*, he found the style of the latter "drawling"[57] and "a poor, threadbare performance" as an allegory;[58] but he praised its "fanciful descriptions of Scenes that have no foundation in Nature or Possibility."[59] In connection with Trumbull's lifelong interest in prosody, he made jottings in his notebook about "the dactylic form"[60] and "the Gothic or Runic alliteration" in Langland's *Vision of Piers Plowman*, and about Shakespeare's mockery of alliteration in the speeches of Pyramus and Thisbe. Except for Trumbull's remarks about Milton, these scattered comments and the numerous references in *An Essay on the Use and Advantages of the Fine Arts* seem to be the only ones extant on the English bards before the eighteenth century.

For a thorough understanding of his views on Milton, one of his favorite poets, more evidence would be necessary; that which exists, nevertheless, is sufficient to indicate that his approach to the English writer was both perceptive and judicial. In a letter of January 8, 1772, Trumbull agreed with Silas Deane, for example, that *Paradise Regained* did not enhance Milton's reputation; but, on the other hand, he thought it had numerous merits and astutely observed, "We are disgusted with it, because it is beneath what we expect from Milton." As a poet, he recognized the greatness of *Paradise Lost* at the same time that he, a staunch Calvinist, thought the doctrines in the poem Arian. But then he did "not look to Poets for creeds of divinity,"[61] he said; and he had little hope for any theological truths in Milton's newly discovered *Treatise on Christian Doctrine*. With considerable insight Trumbull not only defended Milton's use of sin and death as necessary to account for Satan's escape but endorsed the "allegory" as so well done that, despite critics' objections, he would not want it omitted.[62] He explained some of the English poet's language as an expedient adopted because Thomas Rymer and other critics insisted that blank verse was not poetry. To overcome the argument of these men, Trumbull said, "Milton affected Archaisms & Greek or Latin forms of expression."[63] The American poet also observed that the author of *Paradise Lost* knew the Latin idiom better than any other and that the great epic, by modifying the language, had become "far more English, than when it was written."

Another source that reveals Trumbull's standards in verse is his mature ranking of the epic poets, which is noteworthy, perhaps, for the high positions assigned to Milton and to Dwight. The list, arranged in a column in Noah Webster's hand, is as follows: Homer—Milton, Virgil, Tasso, Camoëns, Ariosto, Ossian, Spenser, Dwight, Lucan, Ercilla, Statius, Cowley. Claudian, Voltaire, and Silius Italicus.[64] For the first two men, this order of preference changes the estimate given in the master's oration of 1770, in which the English poet is said to have "produced a Poem, almost as much superior to Homer's, in sublimity of conception, as it is in the greatness of its subject."

Trumbull's basic neo-Classical standards are apparent in his estimates of eighteenth-century English poets and poetry. He thought that Cowley, possessor of "lively imagination & sublime genius,"[65] wrote excellent Latin poems when following his models; but in English he ran to farcical extravagance, as in the description of the angel Gabriel dressing for his mission to David. William Cowper's *Task* he found "perfectly intelligible"[66] but often indistinguishable from prose. He found both virtues and faults in Pope, a writer with whom he has been thought similar in spirit. He agreed with Johnson "that Pope by his Translations of Homer tuned the Public ear,"[67] but he also noted that the bard of Twickenham "gave them but a single tune." Overall, he rated Pope "the greatest master of perfect versification,"[68] a model of "elegance & correctness"[69] and "condensed" style.[70] He regarded Pope as the Virgil and Addison as the Cicero of their time.[71] But Thomson he condemned for the bombast in a blank verse description of a storm in *The Seasons*.

In the essay "On Johnson's Imitations of Juvenal's Satires,"[72] Trumbull used comparisons to highlight faults and virtues. He considered Johnson "more correct and methodical" than Juvenal and superior to the Roman poet "in strength & conciseness of expression" but inferior to him in selecting "some circumstance, which gives the whole idea at a stroke." When Trumbull wrote concerning their total effect, he said, "Let critics praise Johnson, as they will; I am still better pleased with the reading of Juvenal." In this opinion he proved himself no servile follower of his English contemporaries.

As for the Romantic movement, Trumbull, who had been nurtured in religious poetry and schooled in Classicism, was partly at odds with it. Apparently he admired the descriptive verse of Sir Walter Scott,[73] and he granted Thomas Moore's "great method"[74] in describing feminine beauty; also, he praised *The Corsair* as the "most finished"[75] production by Lord Byron. On the other hand, he censured the Romantic poets for faults ranging from dull verses by Robert Southey[76] to the more serious lack of control and morals.

In his negative comments about several poets he exhibited again his neo-Classical criteria; for he complained of the "eccentricity" of Leigh Hunt's *The Story of Rimini*[77] as well as of the "wildness of imagination"[78] of Samuel Taylor Coleridge; and he condemned "the misanthropy of L. Byron, the nauseous impurity of Thos. Moore, the vulgarity of Wordsworth, the silliness of Leigh Hunt & the wild unmeaning rants of Coleridge &c. &c.— &c."[79] In an acid comparison he characterized the work of Coleridge and his associates: "If as though, a poetical Bedlam was about to be erected on the summit of Parnassus, and they were to show themselves qualified for the professorships in that academy."[80] In vivid phrases he compared Moore to "a Boy sorcerer chasing rainbows of his own creation," possessed of a "poetic fire" which was "mostly phosphoric—full of glare & flare, glimmer & glister." And he said Moore "exclaims with his own Peri 'Oh, am I not happy? I am, I am.'" Those strictures were not lightly arrived at, for Trumbull had thoroughly studied the Irish author's writings and had made several pages of quotations in his notebooks. He charged George Crabbe and others with coarseness and wrote, "Instead of endeavoring like their predecessors, to soar to the summit, they employ themselves in digging for gold & diamonds in the caverns & vaults of Parnassus, or bathing in the muddy bottom of the streams of Helicon." And last, applying a moral criterion to Byron and Moore, he castigated the former for excelling "in passion & feeling only— but only of the *worst* sort" and the latter as being "the Poet of Voluptuousness." These faults and others he hoped the *Warreniana* would root out by means of its satirical criticism.

Usually, Trumbull held a more favorable opinion of American poets than he thought the British critics did. Bryant he praised for "correct judgment & classical taste" and for his freedom from *"Byronic* mania."[81] Making an evaluation with which later generations have agreed, he called James Percival a man of genuine ability who had written "much...not above mediocrity."[82] And in a bantering style characteristic of his personal letters, he praised the verse of John Quincy Adams in his letter of April 27, 1793, to John Adams, then ended with the twitting observation that the verse was "very much superior to the general cast of American, & especially *Bostonian* Poetry." Though Trumbull was candid about the verse of his friends, he at times allowed a little too much optimism to enter into his comments. He thought, for example, that much of Barlow's *The Vision of Columbus* had "not been excelled in Sublimity since the days of Milton,"[83] a judgment which long has seemed mistaken.

But friendship did not always distort Trumbull's evaluations, for he was able to see both the strengths and the weaknesses in the verse of Dwight, who he at one time thought would be "our American poet."[84] In 1772, Trumbull defended his friend's use of abbreviations to Silas Deane; and a year later he wrote to Joseph Howe that Dwight was even better as a poet than before.[85] Trumbull was too honest, however, not to perceive faults in his colleague's work. By way of "The Meddler" in 1770 he jocularly pointed out some excesses: "A late Poet has been extremely free in the use of these expedients; for lyons & tygers, one might as well travel in the desarts of *Lybia*: And he hath filled his work with so much thunder & lightning, that upon reading it, I could compare his head to nothing, but Vulcan's shop, in mount Aetna, in which an hundred Cyclops were perpetually employed in forging thunderbolts."[86] In the same vein, after reading the first part of *The Conquest of Canäan*, Trumbull asked Dwight "to send a *lightning rod*"[87] along with the ending to the work.

Fortunately, Noah Webster left a record in his own hand of some "satyrical" comments Trumbull made on Dwight's poem;[88] and President Stiles recorded that on May 20, 1790, he "Spent the Foren. at Mr. Trumbull's in reviewg Dwight's Poem with his Erasures, Criticisms, & satyrical Remarks."[89] Trumbull objected to obscure metaphors, prolixity, ineffective descriptions "in a kind of *glowing patchwork*," insufficient variety of characters, and a special "poetical vocabulary" needing a glossary. Though he qualified his praise on the versification, he did find it generally superior. All in all, he made an honest evaluation of the epic by his lifelong friend.

We do not have his specific suggestions given to Dwight[90] or Lydia H. Sigourney, who "would permit none of her poems to be published which had not been first inspected and revised by Trumbull";[91] but fortunately we have a letter to James Athearn Jones, who had sent his slender volume of verse to the aging Hartford wit. Prefacing his suggestions, Trumbull said an advisor should avoid both "undistinguishing praise"[92] and severe censures on "minute defects." In keeping with these ideas, he lauded Jones for the description of a storm at sea and for blank verse which avoided "labored pomp, monotonous cadences, & diffusive verbosity." On the other hand, he objected to "one or two passages" on moral grounds, and he suggested that the story told by the maniac Madeline should contain more "wild language" in order to be suited to her.

Trumbull placed a lesser value on his own poetical talents than on those of his friends. In 1785, he rated himself inadequate to maintain for any length of time "the Sublime or pathetic Style,"[93] which he admired, just as, a decade earlier, he thought himself incapable of writing extended burlesque.[94] Apparently during his intensive study in Watertown his ideal for poetry changed, as in 1778 he regretted that he had followed too much the inflated epithets, pomposity, and turgid descriptions of English poetry in what he called his "more laboured productions,"[95] presumably such poems as "The Genius of America; An Ode," "An Elegy on the Times," and "Ode to Sleep." Though modest about his powers, he wanted his poems published. In 1773 he contemplated a poetic miscellany with his close friend Dwight,[96] later he made his verse available to Barlow,[97] and in 1785 he wrote to Mathew Carey that he wanted to publish a revised *M'Fingal* and all his other verse "both in the serious and humorous style."[98] In 1797, during his long illness, he was revising his poems;[99] and at last he achieved in 1820 the publication of his collected verse in S. G. Goodrich's two-volume edition.

These miscellaneous remarks on poetry follow the neo-Classical standards which appear also in his published critiques, but they differ in style and in scope. Not designed for publication, they were more informal and uninhibited. And they dealt with the verse not only from Classical times to 1800 but also with that in the Romantic period, some of which was condemned according to a moral yardstick.

III   *Published Literary Criticism*

Trumbull published at least six pieces of literary criticism in addition to the letter to Van Winkle about *Percy's Masque*. Perhaps the least valuable is *An Essay on the Use and Advantages of the Fine Arts*, his master's oration in 1770 and one of the earlier examples of criticism in American literature. Taken as a whole, the speech was a bold performance noteworthy for its defense of studying literature, its perception of the faults in contemporary English writing, and for its patriotism. The fact that it owed much to Kames may have been unavoidable, for in a college in which the study of literature was frowned upon as "trifling amusement," the young man needed to buttress his case with respected authority. When he linked his cause to the "taste for more pure and intellectual pleasures" which God had placed in human minds, he almost certainly was indebted to Kames's idea that "a taste in the fine arts goes hand in hand with the moral sense, to which indeed it is nearly allied."[100] From the Scottish philosopher may have come other ideas also, such as the effect of voluptuousness mentioned in "Standard of Taste," the twenty-fifth chapter of Kames's *Elements of Criticism*.

In the prose section of the speech, Trumbull developed his ideas according to chronology. After linking the fine arts with morality, he said that for centuries literature had helped to conquer the "rugged ferocity of manners" of the uncivilized nations. After briefly tracing the literary history of Greece and Rome, he dwelt upon that of England. He regretted that following the glory of the preceding two centuries there was a lower achievement in his own era because "of that luxurious effeminacy, which hath caused a decay of genius, and introduced a false taste in writing." Against contemporary English authors, whom he regarded as slavish, pedantic imitators, he made a charge which has had some support in later years: "They sacrifice ease and elegance to the affectation of classic correctness, fetter the fancy with the rules of method, and damp all the ardour of aspiring invention." It was America, he thought, which had a bright and glorious future not only in arms and commerce but also in letters. With considerable optimism he predicted, as we have noted, the coming of eminent American authors who would rival or surpass their great English predecessors, including Shakespeare.

Trumbull had a connection with at least the first two parts of Noah Webster's *A Grammatical Institute of the English Language*, one of the first books printed under the protection of the copyright act. For the first part, the famous speller, Trumbull wrote an endorsement on April 28, 1783, in which he stated that he had examined the manuscript and found it superior to Thomas Dilworth's speller and that Robert Lowth's grammar was not suited for use in schools. The significance of the testimonial lies in the two points on which Trumbull said Webster's volume surpassed Dilworth's and other spellers: first, the inclusion of rules of pronunciation; and second, sensible rules for syllabication, for they were the ones which Webster later used in his dictionaries and which are still in force. This statement, with the *I* changed to *we*,[101] appeared on the first page of the Connecticut *Courant* for October 14, 1783, one week after the speller was published. It was signed by Trumbull and eight other men, including Joel Barlow.

For the second part of the *Institute*,[102] Trumbull wrote the section on prosody at the request of Webster, who was living in his house at the time. Trumbull began his essay with a discussion of accent and emphasis. Though he praised Thomas Sheridan's definitions of these terms in the section called "A Rhetorical Grammar" in *A General Dictionary of the English Language* (1780), he offered his own ideas, describing accent as the "stress of the voice, regulated merely by the rule of pronunciation,"[103] and dividing emphasis into "natural" and "accidental." In the essay proper he objected to attempts to base English versification on Latin, he distinguished between long and short syllables, and he illustrated the kinds of poetic feet. At the end, he placed observations on how to read poetry, citing Kames on the "nature of the cesural [*sic*] pause"[104] and Sheridan on "the final pause." In some succeeding editions of Part Two, Webster omitted the section on prosody; but he later restored it, and in 1807 he gave Trumbull credit for his essay.

In addition to the material already mentioned, there are three essays hitherto not attributed to Trumbull. In writing them, he was motivated partly by a reasonable patriotism and partly by his perennial dissatisfaction with incompetent critics but principally by his lifelong friendship with Humphreys, the inscription[105] for whose granite obelisk he, not Benjamin Silliman,[106] was to write a few years later. Just as in "The Correspondent" Trumbull had said that he would defend a friend against slander, so now he supported Humphreys against a belittling and irritating review of his *Miscellaneous Works*[107] which had appeared in the *Monthly Anthology, and Boston Review* for September 1804. This struggling new magazine was edited at the time by Ralph Waldo Emerson's father, the Reverend William Emerson. One of the book reviewers, the Reverend J. S. J. Gardiner, former associate of Dr. Samuel Parr of London, contributed the offensive review, which was condescending in tone, amateurish in method, and inaccurate in facts.

Gardiner began with the frequent assumption on the ages of poetry, followed with disparaging comments on what he called "excellences,"[108] and concluded with "faults" in Humphreys's works. He based the first portion on the cliché that "Poetry is said to flourish, previously to the other arts, in the infancy of society; to attain elegance and correctness in its middle age; and thence, in its decline, to degenerate into the *nugae cemorae* [*canorae*], the tinkling trifles of mere versifyers." He maintained that the history not only of Classical poetry but also that of France and England substantiated the idea; and then he applied it to England. After beginning with Chaucer and granting improvement in the days of Queen Elizabeth, he categorically stated that the English "language was not brought to perfection till the reign of queen Anne, the Augustan age of England, when a host of writers arose of superiour excellence." After insisting that "the age of good English poetry was past,"[109] he contended that American verse was doubly damned because it was closely linked with the decline in England's poetry and because American authors received little financial reward.

Mistaken as these ideas might be, they were less objectionable than the remainder of the review. Except for praising the biography of General Israel Putnam, Gardiner limited Humphreys's merits to his being "an excellent and worthy man,"[110] and "an apparently good and sensible man, and true American,"[111] who could not stand comparison with the British Augustan Age but who made "no mean figure" "on the American Parnassus."[112] Turning to the "faults" next, he objected strongly to placing the accent on the first syllable of words such as *unborn* and *untamed* and quoted a passage from Churchill for illustration. He also objected to placing the stress on adjectives, an accent on the second syllable of *exquisite,* the use of *licit,* and to the syllabication in the name Tyrteus. Along the way he made a gratuitous gibe at Trumbull's friend Noah Webster as one of the "conceited innovators" in language.

Trumbull defended Humphreys in three articles. The first appeared in the *Monthly Anthology, and Boston Review* for December 1804, and the second in the January 1805 issue of the same magazine. The third was printed in the *New-England Palladium* in four consecutive installments, beginning with January 29, 1805. Although the articles in the *Monthly Anthology, and Boston Review* have been attributed to Humphreys,[113] a letter he sent to Trumbull dated February 4, 1805, pointed to the latter as the author. After Humphreys told how he had delivered the second and third essays, he warned Trumbull, "[You] must not expect to escape from the field before the hurly burly is done—and the battle lost or won. . . . You cannot be excused for having begun the conflict bravely & furnished so much ammunition. . . ."[114] The first and the third pieces of "ammunition" were fairly lengthy, but the second was a shorter article which seems like an afterthought to the first. It was characteristic that these essays were anonymous, the first being signed "Harvardiensis" and the others lacking even a pseudonym.

By means of the articles, Trumbull defended the work of his friend Humphreys and, incidentally, gave some hints of what he thought literary criticism should be. Destroying Gardiner's unwarranted strictures, he reduced them to absurdity; he turned them into weapons against the reviewer; or, most often, he proved them erroneous by examples and comparisons. He was honest, for he refused to overpraise Humphreys even though he wanted to encourage American letters.

Insofar as the objectionable article was concerned, Trumbull arrived at a conclusion entirely in accord with the evaluation a modern critic has made concerning Gardiner's reviews in general: "Virtually all that Gardiner derived from Johnson or his Whig imitator Parr was their manner, pompous and rough. He was form without substance."[115] To disprove the points of Gardiner or to turn them back against him, Trumbull drew on his detailed knowledge of literature and on his dialectical skill. Probably because of the reviewer's insistence on British superiority, Trumbull opened the December essay with sarcastic references to his never having gone to a British school or to his even having been in England. Then he attacked the shortcomings of the review itself.

First, Trumbull asked questions, among them one aimed at the reason no summary of Humphreys's *Works* had been given, as was customary in English periodicals. Next, he appropriately asked what "excellences" the reviewer had singled out. Then he defended Humphreys against the alleged "faults" by marshaling overwhelming evidence in support of the colonel's writing. To counter animadversions on accenting the first syllable of words such as *unknown,* Trumbull cited four examples from Milton and one from Pope, noted that the reviewer had mistaken the point in the quotation from Churchill, and pleaded poetic license as well. Pretending to place Humphreys before a British tribunal for adjudication of the point, he listed examples from Watts, C. Pulteney, and Young; and he pointed out that in his dictionary Johnson, citing the works of Milton, Spenser, Fairfax, Shakespeare, and Dryden, listed four examples of *uncouth* accented on the first syllable and two on the ultimate.

Similarly, he answered Gardiner's argument against having the beat fall on the adjective rather than the noun, and he invalidated the point concerning historical accuracy in Humphreys by mentioning the *Iliad,* the *Aeneid,* and *Paradise Lost.* He granted the stricture on the pronunciation of *exquisite,* but he defended the use of *licit* and neatly explained the apparent rhyming of *array'd* and *bride* by referring to the list of errata. After controverting the "faults" with the one exception, he concluded the essay with cutting finality in his recommendation that the reviewer read line 85 in Pope's *Imitations of Horace,* Book II, Satire 1. If Gardiner checked the reference, he found "Its proper pow'r to hurt, each creature feels"; and he could hardly have ignored the line completing the couplet: "Bulls aim their horns, and Asses lift their heels."

To the next issue of the same periodical Trumbull contributed a shorter essay. In it he paraphrased the reviewer's theory of poetic ages, to which he had alluded only briefly in December; and for the first time in the skirmish he pointed to the merits in Humphreys's poems. To do so, he employed comparable passages describing "a realm, once populous and happy, now exhibiting all the marks of ruin and desolation."[116] After quoting from Pope's *Windsor Forest*, Goldsmith's *The Deserted Village*, Trumbull's imitations of Isaiah, Dwight's *The Conquest of Canäan*, and Humphreys's *The Glory of America; or, Peace Triumphant over War*, he asserted that the passage from Humphreys possessed the greatest force, strength, nobility, and sublimity. Then he contended that the American people "quietly endure such contemptuous criticisms"[117] of American poetry as Gardiner's "because, amidst the mutual clamors of contending parties, not one reader in a thousand cares three cents about the poetical or literary honour of his country." With this Federalist and patriotic thrust he concluded his essay.

In the four-part article in the *New-England Palladium* Trumbull surpassed his work in the two essays in the *Monthly Anthology, and Boston Review*. Less caustic than in the first essay but equally clever, learned, and thorough, he not only included the points made in that article (though with different supporting quotations) but added others. Occasionally he was sarcastic, as when he adroitly turned back on the reviewer that man's own method. Because Gardiner had praised Humphreys as a man while damning him as a poet, Trumbull wrote, ". . . I am also willing to declare, that I stand ready to believe that the Reviewer is one of the best and greatest men in the world, in every respect, except the business of reviewing."[118]

In general, however, Trumbull depended on sense and solid learning. With them he exposed the shallowness of the myth of the poetic ages, disproving its appropriateness for Greece, Rome, and France, as well as for England. He listed Johnson's and the London Booksellers' standard authors for Queen Anne's reign and exclaimed, "These are the writers, with whom Dwight, Humphreys, and Barlow are not fit to be compared. Hughes,

Broome, Pomfret, Yalden!"[119] If Pope were excepted, he said, there would not be three authors from the list rising above an "unanimated strain of listless mediocrity."[120]

Furthermore, he argued, the English language had had no standard as such until Johnson's dictionary, a work which together with his other writings fostered "perpetual infusions of pedantic Latinity" and led to "a style . . . unnatural, bombastic and pompous."[121] He also contended that as an "innovator," Webster erred on the side of caution and that Humphreys's allegedly faulty accents were owing to the use of spondees. By this time, at the end of the fourth article, he had exposed the utter incompetence of the reviewer.

Incomplete though the record is, the literary criticism by Trumbull explains why Humphreys wrote to him that the latter had an obligation to "the present age and to posterity" because he possessed "such talents, erudition, and critical knowledge,"[122] and why Noah Webster called Trumbull "the best critic of [his] age."[123] It indicated that Trumbull had the wide knowledge, the articulateness, the thoroughness in examining the minutiae, the candor, and the honesty that are the requisites for sound evaluation of literature. It gives solid evidence for believing that, had the times and circumstances been more propitious, Trumbull could have become our first major American literary critic.

CHAPTER 7

"Service to Mankind"

TRUMBULL stands as a minor poet whose only remaining
works of general interest are *The Progress of Dulness* and
M'Fingal. Not gifted with lyric strength or great versatility in
verse form, he nevertheless did write these two poems which
have survived two centuries. He worked with subject matter
which long ago lost its pertinence for readers, but he penned
such witty, quotable octosyllabic couplets that they still can
be perused with enjoyment.

Though much of Trumbull's work is no longer read, some of
it is of historical importance in American literature. His early
newspaper writings are among the better colonial Addisonian
essays, the initial numbers of "The Correspondent" constitute
the first effective use of satire in Connecticut to quell the raging
theological controversies, and the fragmentary "The Mathematical Metaphysician" is one of the earliest colonial attempts
at a novel. Though of little intrinsic value, the newsboy's addresses are among the best of their kind. The collaborations on
psalms and hymns, a play, and part of Webster's work are of
some importance. The literary criticism, though chauvinistic in
the author's early years, is perceptive and basically sound.

In other ways, too, Trumbull contributed to our literary and
cultural heritage. As an advisor familiar with both ancient and
modern literature, he urged upon authors seeking his guidance
the intelligent application of neo-Classical standards. With
M'Fingal, he helped overcome the young nation's sense of
inferiority in the arts. He contributed skillful political prose
which was published or reprinted in other states as well as in
Connecticut during the Revolutionary and early National periods.
In revising Humphreys's version of Washington's last circular

151

letter to the governors, one of the General's critically important documents, Trumbull did his country a great service. He wrote articles marked by their patriotic and Federalistic leanings, some of them being informational, and others, like "Mother Carey's Chickens," being bitingly satirical. The acknowledged leader of the "Hartford Wits," he played an important role in the production of the well-known *Anarchiad* and urged adoption of the Constitution in other writings as well. No final estimate of the worth of his prose propaganda can yet be given because it is still being identified, but that which is known suggests a mighty pen whose worth is considerably greater than has heretofore been suspected.

In seeking "honor" for himself and "service to mankind,"[1] Trumbull made a solid minor literary achievement; and he had the potential for an even greater one. Though early in life he had hoped for a career in poetry and is indeed known to us mainly for his two verse satires, he was in many ways better suited to prose, in which he often was masterly, whether in his essays, his political propaganda, or his scintillating letters, particularly those to John Adams. Learned, brilliant, literate, and courageous, Trumbull leaves us with tantalizing thoughts of what, in more favorable times, he might have accomplished in light verse, in prose and verse satire, and, especially, in literary criticism.

Notes and References

Chapter One

1. John Trumbull, ["While You, my Friend, to Flow'ry meads resort"], Moses Coit Tyler Collection, Cornell University Library, hereafter cited as Cornell MSS.

2. [John Trumbull], "Memoir of the Author," in *The Poetical Works of John Trumbull, LL.D.* (Hartford, 1820), I, 9. Subsequent references to this will appear as "Memoir."

3. *Extracts from the Itineraries and Other Miscellanies of Ezra Stiles, D.D., LL.D., 1775-1794,* ed. Franklin B. Dexter (New Haven, 1916), p. 400. Other material in this and the immediately succeeding paragraphs on his reading and preparation for college are drawn from the same source.

4. Cornell MSS.

5. The two poems and the translation cited in this paragraph are in the Cornell MSS.

6. Alexander Cowie, *John Trumbull: Connecticut Wit* (Chapel Hill, 1936), p. 40.

7. "Juvenilia," Cornell MSS.

8. Draft of a letter (never sent) from William Whitman to Lydia H. Sigourney, William Woodbridge Papers in the Burton Historical Collection of the Detroit Public Library, hereafter referred to as Burton MSS.

9. Trumbull to John Adams, March 14, 1790, the Adams Papers, Massachusetts Historical Society, microfilm ed. (hereafter referred to as APm), reel #373.

10. Cornell MSS.

11. *Ibid.*

12. *Ibid.*

13. Cowie, p. 46.

14. Cornell MSS. Listed by Leon Howard, *The Connecticut Wits* (Chicago, 1943), in his "A Check List," p. 414, as published by Cowie, who, however, did not include the last fifteen lines. Cowie, p. 45.

15. Burton MSS.

16. Cowie, p. 48.

17. Cornell MSS.

18. Some of the punctuation and capitalization has been normalized.

19. Manuscript copies are in the Burton MSS and in the Beinecke Rare Book and Manuscript Library of the Yale University Library.

20. Burton MSS.

21. Cowie, p. 49, n. 60; *The Columbian Magazine, or Monthly Miscellany*, III, 6 (June 1789), 373-78; *The Monthly Anthology, and Boston Review*, II, 5 (May 1805), 247-50; *The Port Folio*, V, 40 (October 1805), 319-21; Evert A. and George L. Duyckinck, *Cyclopaedia of American Literature* (New York, 1855), I, 312-14.

22. *Poetical Works*, II, 131.

23. Cornell MSS.

24. "Original Communications," *The Monthly Magazine, and British Register*, VI, 35 (August 1798), 81-82.

25. "Critical Reflections," October 1778, Cornell MSS.

26. Burton MSS. Lines Cowie did not include.

27. Burton MSS.

28. *Ibid.*

29. *Poetical Works*, II, 171. Cowie, p. 70.

30. *Poetical Works*, II, 187.

31. *Ibid.*, p. 165.

32. *The Superior Court Diary of William Samuel Johnson, 1772-1773*, ed. John T. Farrell, American Legal Records, IV (Washington, D.C., 1942), 56.

33. Cornell MSS.

34. See his condemnation of slander in "The Correspondent," No. XVIII, *The Connecticut Journal, and the New-Haven Post-Boy*, No. 287 (April 16, 1773), p. 1.

35. Burton MSS.

36. Clare I. Cogan, "John Trumbull, Satirist," *The Colonnade*, XIV (1919-1922), 89.

37. In the *Poetical Works*, II, 154.

38. Cornell MSS.

39. *Ibid.* Cowie, p. 128, n. 8.

40. *Poetical Works*, II, 205.

41. Cornell MSS. Cowie published the first parts only of "To a Lady . . ." and "[E]pistle [Addres]s[ed] to Mr I. J." and excerpts from "Epistle to ———." Howard in his "A Check List" includes these as having been published by Cowie.

42. See Trumbull's two letters to Miss Sally Lloyd of Stamford, dated September 10 and November 14, 1773, Hillhouse Family Papers, Yale University Library.

43. *Poetical Works*, II, 113.

44. *Ibid.*, 141. H. W. Starr, "Trumbull and Gray's *Bard*," *Modern Language Notes*, LXII (February 1947), 116-19.

45. *Poetical Works,* II, 195.
46. Cornell MSS.
47. *Poetical Works,* II, 123.
48. Cornell MSS.
49. Cowie, p. 142.
50. Cornell MSS.
51. *Poetical Works,* II, 105 ("Lines Addressed to Messrs. Dwight and Barlow"). The first 26 lines of the 50 total are in the Cornell MSS.
52. Cornell MSS.
53. "For the Statesman & Republican," *Independent Statesman & Maine Republican,* III, 1 (Portland, Maine, July 12, 1823), 1.
54. Howard, p. 415 ("A Check List").
55. Mason Fitch Cogswell, Correspondence and Papers in the Beinecke Rare Book and Manuscript Library, Yale University Library.
56. Noah Webster, "Manuscript Bibliography of the Writings of N. Webster By Himself," *Websteriana: A Catalogue of Books by Noah Webster, Collated from the Library of Gordon L. Ford* (Brooklyn, 1882).
57. "A Poetical Letter: From Lovesick Jacob to Coy Nancy," *The Port Folio,* IV, 28 (1804), 224.

Chapter Two

1. Letter from Trumbull to Deane, May 27, 1775, APm, reel #344.
2. "Memoir," I, 12.
3. Quotations are from *The Boston Chronicle* unless indicated otherwise. Arabic numerals were used in the newspaper, but Roman numerals will be used in the text. Cornell has manuscripts numbered I, II, V, VII, VIII, and X.
4. Howard, p. 41.
5. John E. Alden, "John Mein: Scourge of Patriots," *Publications of the Colonial Society of Massachusetts,* XXXIV (Boston, 1943), 571.
6. Stiles, *Itineraries,* p. 400.
7. *The Spectator,* ed. Donald F. Bond (Oxford, 1965), I, 4. Subsequent references to *The Spectator* are to this edition.
8. *The Tatler,* ed. George A. Aitken (London, 1898), II, 388. Subsequent references to *The Tatler* are to this edition, 1898, 1899.
9. Howard, p. 41.
10. Cowie, p. 54.
11. Richmond P. Bond, *The Tatler* (Cambridge, Massachusetts, 1971), p. 213.
12. "The Correspondent," *The Connecticut Journal, and the New-Haven Post-Boy,* February 23 to July 6, 1770, *passim.* Quotations are from this newspaper, hereafter referred to as *The Connecticut*

Journal in the text and notes. Arabic numerals were used for one through eight, but Roman numerals will be used for the sake of uniformity.

13. MS background essay for "The Correspondent."

14. *Ibid.*

15. Cogan, p. 83.

16. L. D. Turner, "John Trumbull's 'The Correspondent,' No. 8," *The Journal of Negro History*, XIV, 4 (October 1929), 380-81, 493-95.

17. *The Connecticut Journal.* The second group is not in manuscript.

18. Cornell MSS.

19. "The Correspondent," No. 2, Cornell MSS (note).

Chapter Three

1. *The Poetical Works of John Trumbull, LL.D.* (Hartford, 1820), II, 9-90. Quotations are from this edition except for those taken from the Preface to Part II.

2. Stokes Autograph Collection, Yale University Library.

3. Jonathan Swift, *A Tale of a Tub,* eds. A. C. Guthkelch and D. Nichol Smith, 2nd ed. (London, 1958), p. 4.

4. *Ibid.,* p. 7.

5. Letter from Trumbull to Deane, March 28, 1772, The Historical Society of Pennsylvania. No portion of this letter has been previously published.

6. Cowie, p. 114.

7. Howard, p. 54.

8. *Poetical Works,* II, 9-10.

9. "Memoir," I, 12.

10. *The Literary Diary of Ezra Stiles, D.D., LL.D.,* ed. Franklin Bowditch Dexter (New York, 1901), II, 387-88.

11. Howard, p. 56.

12. Timothy Dwight, S.T.D., LL.D., "Introduction," *Theology; Explained and Defended in a Series of Sermons; With a Memoir of the Life of the Author . . . Middletown, Connecticut* (New Haven, 1818-19), I, xi.

13. *The Progress of Dulness, Part Second* ([New Haven], 1773), Preface.

14. Guthkelch and Smith, p. 4.

15. Cowie, p. 118.

16. Letter from Joseph Howe to Trumbull, February 26, 1773, Burton MSS.

17. Samuel Kettell, *Specimens of American Poetry, with Critical and Biographical Notices* (Boston, 1829), I, 178-79.

18. Samuel L. Knapp, *Lectures on American Literature, with Remarks on Some Passages of American History* ([New York], 1829), p. 165.

19. *The American Annual Register for the Year 1831-32*, VII, 383 (Appendix).

20. Review of *The Poets and Poetry of America*, by Rufus Wilmot Griswold, 16th ed., 1855, in *The North American Review*, LXXXII (January 1856), 241.

21. Evert A. and George L. Duyckinck, I, 324.

22. F[rederick] Sheldon, "The Pleiades of Connecticut," *Atlantic Monthly*, XV (February 1865), 191.

23. Howard, p. 54.

24. Cowie, p. 121.

Chapter Four

1. *The Poetical Works of John Trumbull, LL.D.* (Hartford, 1820), I. This edition is used for quotations and as a basis for statistics unless otherwise noted.

2. Fragment of a letter from Trumbull to Adams or Howe, February 17, 1775, Burton MSS.

3. *An Essay on the Use and Advantages of the Fine Arts* (New Haven, [1770]).

4. "The Correspondent," No. IX, *The Connecticut Journal*, No. 278 (February 12, 1773), p. 1.

5. *Ibid.*, No. XVI, No. 285 (April 2, 1773), p. 1.

6. Letter from Abigail Adams to Mercy Otis Warren, ante February 27, 1774 in *Adams Family Correspondence, December 1761-May 1776*, ed. L. H. Butterfield *et al.*, 2nd series (Cambridge, Massachusetts, 1963), I, 98.

7. *Diary and Autobiography of John Adams*, ed. L. H. Butterfield *et al.*, 1st series (Cambridge, Massachusetts, 1961), II, 86.

8. William Woodbridge, *An Address Before the Detroit Young Men's Society, Delivered by Request, April, 1848* (Detroit, 1849), p. 22 (Note). The manuscript of approximately three-fourths of the concluding note is in the Burton MSS titled "Fragment of obituary of John Trumbull, by William Woodbridge."

9. "Memoir," p. 16.

10. Woodbridge, p. 22.

11. "Memoir," p. 17.

12. *Ibid.*

13. Draft of a letter from Trumbull to C. A. Goodrich, August 1823, Burton MSS.

14. J. Hammond Trumbull's annotated copy of Patten's 1782 edition of *M'Fingal*, p. 53, n. 2, The Connecticut Historical Society.

15. The poem was printed also as a fifteen-page pamphlet in 1775 by S. Green, New Haven.

16. Letter from Trumbull to Deane, May 27, 1775.

17. Cowie, p. 133.

18. Cogan, p. 94.

19. Cowie, p. 140.

20. No portion of this letter has been previously published.

21. J. Hammond Trumbull, *The Origin of M'Fingal* (Morrisania, New York, 1868).

22. Fragment of a letter from Trumbull to Adams or Howe, February 17, 1775.

23. *Poetical Works*, II, 231 (Appendix).

24. *Ibid.*, I, 17.

25. "The Deane Papers," I, 86-90, *Collections of the New-York Historical Society for the Year 1886* (New York, 1887).

26. Woodbridge, p. 23.

27. Letter from Trumbull to Deane, October 20, 1775.

28. J. Hammond Trumbull's longhand copy of the poem, with his notes and identifications of the fifty lines later incorporated in *M'Fingal*, is in The Connecticut Historical Society.

29. Letter from John Adams to Trumbull, November 5, 1775, Andre deCoppet Collection of American Historical Manuscripts, Manuscripts Division, Princeton University Library.

30. Letter from Trumbull to John Adams, November 14, 1775, APm, reel #345.

31. "Memoir," I, 17.

32. Woodbridge, p. 23.

33. Stiles, *Itineraries*, p. 401.

34. Letter from Trumbull to the Marquis de Chastellux, May 20, 1785 in *Poetical Works*, II, 231 (Appendix).

35. *M'Fingal: A Modern Epic Poem. Canto First, or The Town-Meeting* (Philadelphia, 1776).

36. Letter from Trumbull to John Adams, November 14, 1775.

37. These pages and lines in the Patten edition follow the order given in the text: p. 5, 11. 63-64; p. 6, 11. 95-98; p. 22, 1. 674; p. 32, 1. 304 ff.; p. 50, 11. 121-22; p. 63, 1. 583; p. 51, 11. 151-52.

38. Quotations in this paragraph are from "Critical Reflections," Cornell MSS.

39. *Poetical Works*, I, 123, n.

40. See J. Hammond Trumbull's annotated edition, p. 4, n. 1.

41. Benson J. Lossing, "Notes" to the 1860 edition of *M'Fingal* (New York, 1860), p. 173.

42. *Adams Family Correspondence*, I, 350.

43. See George Dudley Seymour, *Documentary Life of Nathan*

Hale, Comprising All Available Official and Private Documents Bearing on the Life of the Patriot (New Haven, 1941), p. 274.

44. Letter from Jeremiah Wadsworth to Nathanael Greene, July 10, 1782, Jeremiah Wadsworth Autograph Letters, 1779-1785, Wadsworth Atheneum. Letter from Humphreys to Nathanael Greene, September 24, 1782, Stokes Autograph Collection, Yale University Library.

45. Letter from Greene to Wadsworth, December 21, 1872, Governor Joseph Trumbull Collection, Vol. II, Connecticut State Library.

46. Fragment of a letter, Greene to Trumbull, January 22, 1780, Burton MSS. Letter from Greene to Wadsworth, October 15, 1780, Greene Papers, The Huntington Library. Letter from Greene to Wadsworth, April 21, 1783, Connecticut State Library. See letter from Greene to Knox, July 18, 1781, Greene Papers, The Connecticut Historical Society, cited in Theodore Thayer, *Nathanael Greene: Strategist of the Revolution* (New York, 1960), p. 367.

47. Letter from Nathanael Greene to Trumbull, September 29, 1782, Burton MSS.

48. Letter from Aaron Burr to Jeremiah Wadsworth, October 6, 1782, Wadsworth Autograph Letters.

49. *The Papers of James Madison*, August 1, 1782–December 31, 1782, eds. William T. Hutchinson and William M. E. Rachal, V (Chicago, 1967), 267.

50. *Ibid.*, p. 341.

51. *Ibid.*, p. 319.

52. *The Papers of Alexander Hamilton* (1790-1791), eds. Harold C. Syrett and Jacob E. Cooke, VII (New York, 1963), 167.

53. Letter from John Adams to Trumbull, April 28, 1785, APm, reel #350. This letter was first printed in *The Historical Magazine*, IV (New York, 1860), 195.

54. Letter from Trumbull to John Adams, December 8, 1785, APm, reel #366.

55. Cornell MSS.

56. See Marcus A. Mc Corison, *Vermont Imprints, 1778-1820* (Worcester, 1963).

57. London edition of *M'Fingal*, 1792, Burton Historical Collection.

58. Howard, p. 289.

59. Charles Burr Todd, *Life and Letters of Joel Barlow, LL.D.* (New York, 1886), p. 290.

60. *Bibliography of American Literature*, comp. Jacob Blanck (New Haven, 1955), I, 874.

61. Letter from Joel Barlow to James Watson, August 2, 1792, Clifton Waller Barrett Library of the University of Virginia Library.

62. "Memoir," p. 19.

63. New York edition of *M'Fingal*, 1795, printed for John Buel, No. 132, Fly-Market.

64. Cowie, p. 187, n. 74.

65. *A Collection of Papers on Political, Literary and Moral Subjects* (New York, 1843), pp. 174-75. See also a letter from John Eliot to Jeremy Belknap, March 13, 1783 in *Collections of the Massachusetts Historical Society*, IV, 6th series (Boston, 1891), 247-50 and *The Memorial History of Hartford County, Connecticut, 1633-1884*, ed. J. Hammond Trumbull (Boston, 1886), I, 157, n. 2.

66. George C. Rogers, Jr., *Exhibition of a Federalist: William Loughton Smith of Charleston, 1758-1812* (Columbia, South Carolina, 1962), p. 215.

67. *Poetical Works*, II, 229-30.

68. J. P. Brissot de Warville, *Nouveau Voyage dans Les États-Unis de L'Amérique Septentrionale, Fait en 1788* (Paris, 1791), I, 131.

69. Francisco de Miranda, *The New Democracy in America: Travels of Francisco de Miranda in the United States, 1783-84*, trans. Judson P. Wood; ed. John S. Ezell (Norman, Oklahoma, 1963), p. 116.

70. Letter from Lonson Nash to William Woodbridge, May 25, 1804, Burton MSS.

71. *"M'Fingal Dinner," The Connecticut Courant*, LX, 3104 (July 20, 1824), "*From the New-York American*, July 16."

72. News item, *The Hartford Daily Courant*, XXVII, 289 (December 9, 1863), 2.

73. See, for example, *The Massachusetts Centinel*, VIII, 31 (January 2, 1788), 122; No. 38 (January 26, 1788), 152.

74. Mason Fitch Cogswell, "An Accurate Journal of a Voyage up the North River—In a letter to a friend," Cogswell Papers.

75. "Catalogue of New Publications, Poetical and Dramatic," *The Gentleman's Magazine and Historical Chronicle*, XLVI (1776), 374.

76. "Monthly Catalogue. Poetry," *The Critical Review: or, Annals of Literature*, 1st Ser., XLI (June 1776), 481.

77. "Monthly Catalogue, Poetical," *The Monthly Review: or Literary Journal*, 1st Ser., LIV (June 1776), 504.

78. "Poetical," *The Critical Review: or, Annals of Literature*, 2nd Ser., VI (December 1792), 466.

79. "Art. V. M'Fingal: a modern Epic Poem in Four Cantos," *The Monthly Review; or Literary Journal*, Enl., X (January 1793), 45.

80. "Original Communications," *The Monthly Magazine, and British Register*, VI, 35 (August 1798), 82.

81. "American Writers," *Blackwood's Edinburgh Magazine*, XVII, 97 (February 1825), 202.

82. [Lemuel Hopkins], "Miscellaneous thoughts on the *Poems* of

Mess'rs. *Dwight* and *Barlow*," *The American Mercury*, V, 216 (August 25, 1788), 2.

83. David Ramsay, *The History of the American Revolution* (London, 1793), II, 322.

84. "Hindu Philosopher," *Literary Tablet*, I, 6 (October 13, 1803), 1.

85. Kettell, p. 179.

86. Letter from Elihu White to Woodbridge, May 26, 1834, Burton MSS.

87. Timothy Flint, "Sketches of the Literature of the States," in *The Athenaeum: Journal of Literature, Science, and the Fine Arts* (1835), p. 819.

88. "McFingal," *Southern Literary Messenger*, VII (April 1841), 321-24.

89. See Cowie, p. 197.

90. Rufus Wilmot Griswold, *The Poets and Poetry of America* (Philadelphia, 1842), p. 36.

91. Charles W. Everest, *The Poets of Connecticut* (Hartford, 1843), p. 38.

92. "John Trumbull," Evert A. and George L. Duyckinck, I, 322.

93. Peabody, p. 241.

94. Sheldon, p. 192.

95. Edmund Clarence Stedman, *Poets of America* (Boston, 1885), p. 35.

96. William Bradley Otis, *American Verse, 1625-1807* (New York, 1909), p. 102.

97. Alexander Cowie, "John Trumbull as Revolutionist," *American Literature*, III (November 1931), 287-95.

98. See Henry Seidel Canby, *Classic Americans* (New York, 1959), p. 65.

99. Bruce Ingham Granger, "Hudibras in the American Revolution," *American Literature*, XXVII, 4 (January 1956), 508.

100. *The Satiric Poems of John Trumbull: The Progress of Dulness and M'Fingal*, ed. Edwin T. Bowden (Austin, Texas, 1962).

101. James T. Babb, *White House Library List* (August 9, 1963), p. 1.

Chapter Five

1. Vernon Louis Parrington, ed., "Introduction," *The Connecticut Wits* (New York, 1926), p. xxxviii.

2. Letter from Trumbull to John Adams, December 8, 1785.

3. Letter from Lemuel Hopkins to Oliver Wolcott, Jr., June 28, 1795, Oliver Wolcott, Jr. MSS, The Connecticut Historical Society.

4. Letter from Trumbull to John Adams, January 16, 1794, APm, reel #377.

5. See Cowie, p. 208.

6. "Nomination for members of Congress," *The Connecticut Courant*, XXVIII, 1504 (November 18, 1793), 3.

7. Howard, p. 78.

8. Letter from William Moseley Holland to Park Benjamin, February 9, 1836, John Trumbull Collection, Yale University Library.

9. Letter from Noah Webster to James Kent, October 20, 1804 in *Noah Webster*, ed. Harry R. Warfel (New York, 1953), p. 259.

10. Letter from Trumbull to John Adams, July 21, 1805 (misdated 1801), APm, reel #401.

11. Letter from John Adams to Trumbull, July 27, 1805, APm, reel #118.

12. *The Writings of George Washington from the Original Manuscript Sources, 1745-1799*, ed. John C. Fitzpatrick, XXVI (January 1, 1783–June 10, 1783) (Washington, 1938), pp. 485-86.

13. "To the President of the United States," *The Connecticut Courant*, XXVIII, 1491 (August 19, 1793), 3.

14. This poem was published in *The Connecticut Courant*, No. 1153 (February 26, 1787), p. 3, but Goodrich mistakenly placed it in 1810. See S. G. Goodrich, *Recollections of a Lifetime, or Men and Things I Have Seen* (New York, 1857), II, 116.

15. Trumbull, J. Hammond, "Humphreys' Fable of the Monkey," *The Historical Magazine*, V, 8 (August 1861), 254.

16. A review of *The Anarchiad* edited by Luther G. Riggs (1861) by J. Hammond Trumbull in *The Hartford Daily Courant*, August 1, 1861.

17. Howard, p. 414 (A Check List).

18. A poetical letter, *The Connecticut Courant*, No. 1133 (October 9, 1786), p. 2, copy in The New York Public Library.

19. Theodore Albert Zunder, *The Early Days of Joel Barlow, a Connecticut Wit* (New Haven, 1934), p. 198.

20. Frank Landon Humphreys, *Life and Times of David Humphreys* (New York, 1917), I, 398.

21. See "Introduction," *The Anarchiad: A New England Poem* (1786-1787), written in concert by David Humphreys, Joel Barlow, John Trumbull and Dr. Lemuel Hopkins. Edited in 1861 by Luther G. Riggs. A Facsimile Reproduction with an Introduction and Index by William K. Bottorff (Gainesville, Florida, 1967), pp. ix, x.

22. Knapp, p. 165.

23. Goodrich, II, 115.

24. See Cowie, pp. 209-10.

25. Letter from Trumbull to Jeremiah Wadsworth, February 9,

1793, Connecticut State Library (copy from Wadsworth Atheneum, Wadsworth Autograph Letters).

26. Letter from Trumbull to John Adams, February 25, 1793, APm, reel #376.

27. Everest, p. 94.

28. *Doctor Watts's Imitation of the Psalms of David, Corrected and Enlarged. To which is added a Collection of Hymns* (Hartford, 1785).

29. Howard, p. 161.

30. William K. Bottorff and Arthur L. Ford, eds., *The Works of Joel Barlow*. With Introduction. 2 vols. (Gainesville, Florida, 1970), p. viii.

31. Letter from Trumbull to Jeremiah Wadsworth, July 26, 1779, The Connecticut Historical Society.

32. Letter from Trumbull to John Adams, March 14, 1790.

33. Letter from Woodbridge to Col. John Trumbull, May 20, 1831, Burton MSS.

34. Pierrepont Edwards, according to Howard, p. 203.

35. These three poems are found in the Cornell MSS.

36. *The News-Carrier's Address to His Customers* (Hartford, January 1, 1783); [*The News-Carrier's*] *Address to the Gentlemen and Ladies that he supplies with the "Freeman's Chronicle"* (Hartford, January 1, 1784); *Address of the Carrier of the "Connecticut Courant," to His Patrons* (Hartford, January 1, 1824); manuscript copy of the "Address of the Carrier of the *Connecticut Courant,* to His Patrons," printed in *The Connecticut Courant* (January 4, 1825), Burton MSS.

37. "The Late Judge Trumbull," *Democratic Free Press and Michigan Intelligencer,* I, 3 (May 19, 1831), 3.

38. See letter from Trumbull to John Adams, February 6, 1790.

39. Letter from Trumbull to John Adams, April 27, 1793, APm, reel #376.

40. Letter from Trumbull to John Adams, February 5, 1791.

41. The series ran in the issues of January 7, 14, 21, and 28; February 4 and 11; and April 15.

42. Letter from John Adams to Trumbull, March 18, 1793, Andre deCoppet Collection, Princeton University Library.

43. "The American," *The Connecticut Courant,* XXVIII, 1459 (January 7, 1793), 1.

44. *Ibid.,* No. 1460 (January 14, 1793), 1.

45. *Ibid.,* No. 1461 (January 21, 1793) 1, and No. 1462 (January 28, 1793), 1.

46. *Ibid.,* No. 1463 (February 4, 1793), 1.

47. *Ibid.,* No. 1464 (February 11, 1793), 3.

48. *Ibid.*, No. 1473 (April 15, 1793), 1.

49. Letter from John Adams to Trumbull, January 31, 1793, Andre deCoppet Collection, Princeton University Library.

50. "For the *Gazette of the United States*," *Gazette of the United States*, IV, 91 (April 13, 1793), 363.

51. Richard J. Purcell, *Connecticut in Transition: 1775-1818* (Washington, D.C., 1918), pp. 359-60, n. 54; p. 414, n. 47.

52. *Biographical Sketch of the Character of Governor Trumbull*, p. 9.

53. See his copy in The Connecticut Historical Society.

54. [Fourth-of-July address], Burton MSS.

Chapter Six

1. Alexander Cowie, "John Trumbull Glances at Fiction," *American Literature*, XII (March 1940), 69.

2. Alexander Cowie, "John Trumbull as a Critic of Poetry," *New England Quarterly*, XI (December 1938), 773.

3. Letter from William Moseley Holland to Park Benjamin, February 9, 1836.

4. See letter from Abigail Adams to John Adams, November 16, 1788, APm, reel #371 and a letter from William S. Shaw to Abigail Adams, October 3, 1799, APm, reel #396.

5. "Juvenilia," Cornell MSS.

6. Letter from Trumbull to John Adams, February 6, 1790.

7. Quoted by Elkanah Watson in "Preface," *Tour in Holland in MDCCLXXXIV* (Worcester, Massachusetts, 1790), p. viii.

8. "The Correspondent," No. 2, Cornell MSS.

9. Miscellaneous notes, Burton MSS.

10. Essay dated August 1781, Cornell MSS.

11. Miscellaneous notes, Burton MSS. William Gifford, ed., *The Anti-Jacobin; or, Weekly Examiner*, No. 1-36 (November 20, 1797–July 9, 1798); Horace and James Smith, *Rejected Addresses: or, the New Theatrum Poetarum* (London, 1812); *Warreniana; with Notes, Critical and Explanatory*, by the Editor of a Quarterly Review ... (London, 1824).

12. Max F. Schulz, "John Trumbull and Satirical Criticism of Literature," *Modern Language Notes*, LXXIII (February 1958), 85.

13. "The Meddler," No. VII, *The Boston Chronicle*, II, 51, 155 (December 18 to December 21, 1769), 410.

14. Letter from Holland to Benjamin, February 9, 1836.

15. *Ibid.*

16. "The Meddler," No. X, *The Boston Chronicle*, III, 4, 164 (January 18 to January 22, 1770), 25.

17. Miscellaneous notes, Burton MSS.

18. Noah Webster, *A Collection of Essays and Fugitiv Writings on Moral, Historical, Political and Literary Subjects* (Boston, 1790), p. 252. Others on pp. 222, 251-52.

19. *Ibid.*, p. 259.

20. Letter from Trumbull to S. Converse, March 28, 1826 in *New-York Evening Post*, No. 7439 (May 17, 1826), p. 2.

21. Lord Kames (Henry Home), *Elements of Criticism*, ed. Abraham Mills, New ed. (New York, 1854), pp. 391-413.

22. Hugh Blair, D.D., F.R.S., *Lectures on Rhetoric and Belles Lettres*, ed. Abraham Mills (Philadelphia, 1851), p. 452.

23. Kames, pp. 50-58.

24. Letter from Holland to Benjamin, February 9, 1836.

25. See Cowie, "John Trumbull Glances at Fiction," p. 69.

26. "Perfection here below," Burton MSS.

27. "On Romances and Novels," Cornell MSS.

28. Found in a verse letter called "Epistle to ——," Cornell MSS.

29. Letter from Holland to Benjamin, February 9, 1836.

30. "American Literary Intelligence," *The Monthly Anthology, and Boston Review*, IV, 11 (November 1807), 625.

31. Letter from Trumbull to Jedidiah Morse, February 14, 1791, Pennsylvania Historical Society, Philadelphia.

32. Watson, p. vii.

33. *Men and Times of the Revolution; or Memoirs of Elkanah Watson . . . from 1777-1842*, ed. Winslow C. Watson (New York, 1856), p. 131.

34. Francis Le Vaillant, *New Travels into the Interior Parts of Africa*, trans. (London, 1796).

35. Mauritius Benyowsky, *Memoirs and Travels of Mauritius Augustus, Count de Benyowsky* (London, 1790).

36. Miscellaneous notes, Burton, MSS.

37. Letter from Trumbull to John Adams, June 5, 1790, APm, reel #373.

38. "The American," No. II in *The Connecticut Courant*, XXVIII, 1460 (January 14, 1793), 1. See also letter from Trumbull to John Adams, March 30, 1790, APm, reel #373.

39. Letter from Trumbull to John Adams, March 20, 1791, APm, reel #374.

40. See Charles Tabb Hazelrigg, *American Literary Pioneer: A Biographical Study of James A. Hillhouse* (New York, 1953), p. 65.

41. *An Essay on the Use and Advantages of the Fine Arts*, p. 9.

42. "Juvenilia," Cornell MSS.

43. Trumbull's "Extract to Jas. A. Hillhouse," Cornell MSS.

44. Noah Webster, Jun. Esq., *A Grammatical Institute of the English Language, Part II* (Hartford, 1784), p. 130.

45. Extract to James Hillhouse.

46. Letter from Trumbull to James A. Hillhouse, March 1818, Hillhouse Family Papers, Yale University Library. Subsequent quotations in this paragraph are from the same source.

47. Letter from Trumbull to Hillhouse, May 16, 1825, Hillhouse Family Papers.

48. James A. Hillhouse, *Dramas, Discourses, and Other Pieces* (Boston, 1839), II, dedicatory page.

49. "The Meddler," No. X, in the manuscript only, Cornell MSS.

50. Miscellaneous notes, Burton MSS.

51. Letter from Holland to Benjamin, February 9, 1836.

52. "The Meddler," No. X, manuscript only.

53. Letter from Trumbull to James A. Jones, December 12, 1820, "A Letter of John Trumbull," Katherine A. Conley, *New England Quarterly*, XI (June 1938), 372-74.

54. Miscellaneous notes, Burton MSS.

55. Letter from Holland to Benjamin, February 9, 1836.

56. "The Meddler," No. X, manuscript only.

57. Letter from Trumbull to Deane, January 8, 1772.

58. "On Romances and Novels," Cornell MSS.

59. *Ibid.*

60. Miscellaneous notes, Cornell MSS.

61. Letter from Trumbull to Lydia H. Sigourney, March 22, 1826, The Connecticut Historical Society.

62. "The Meddler," No. X, Cornell MSS.

63. Extract to Hillhouse.

64. Noah Webster Papers, Manuscript Division, The New York Public Library, Astor, Lenox and Tilden Foundations.

65. Miscellaneous notes, Burton MSS.

66. Extract to Hillhouse.

67. Miscellaneous notes, Cornell MSS.

68. Letter from Holland to Benjamin, February 9, 1836.

69. Letter from Trumbull to Jones, December 12, 1820.

70. Extract to Hillhouse.

71. "Critical Reflections," Cornell MSS.

72. *Ibid.*

73. Letter from Holland to Benjamin, February 9, 1836.

74. Miscellaneous notes, Burton MSS.

75. Letter from Holland to Benjamin, February 9, 1836.

76. Letter from Trumbull to Hillhouse, May 16, 1825.

77. Letter from Trumbull to Jones, December 12, 1820.

78. Miscellaneous notes, Cornell MSS.

79. "Warreniana," Burton MSS.

80. This and the following quotations in the paragraph are in miscellaneous notes in the Cornell MSS.

81. Letter from Trumbull to Hillhouse, May 16, 1825.

82. Letter from Holland to Benjamin, February 8, 1836.

83. Letter from Trumbull to John Adams, December 8, 1785.

84. Letter from Trumbull to Deane, January 8, 1772. See also letter from Trumbull to Deane, March 8, 1772.

85. Letter from Trumbull to Joseph Howe, February 9, 1773, Burton MSS.

86. "The Meddler," No. X, Cornell MSS.

87. Kettell, p. 176, n.

88. Noah Webster, "Remarks on the stile of the Conquest of Canaan," Manuscript Division, The New York Public Library, Astor, Lenox and Tilden Foundations.

89. Stiles, *Diary*, III, 394.

90. "Memoir," p. 15.

91. "John Trumbull," *Pioneer Collections: Report of the Pioneer Society of the State of Michigan*, 2nd ed., II (1901), 56. See also a letter from Lydia H. Sigourney to Juliana Woodbridge, June 18, 1839, Burton MSS.

92. Letter from Trumbull to Jones, December 12, 1820.

93. Letter from Trumbull to John Adams, December 8, 1785.

94. Letter from Trumbull to Deane, May 27, 1775.

95. "Critical Reflections," Cornell MSS.

96. Fragment of a letter from Trumbull to Howe, February 9, 1773.

97. Letter from Barlow to Greene, March 21, 1784, Stokes Autograph Collection, Yale University Library.

98. Letter from Trumbull to Mathew Carey, June 4, 1785 in *Passages from the Correspondence and Other Papers of Rufus W. Griswold* (Cambridge, Massachusetts, 1898), pp. 8-9.

99. Letter to Trumbull from John Adams, January 19, 1797, APm, reel #117.

100. Kames, p. 13.

101. Noah Webster Papers, Manuscript Division, The New York Public Library, Astor, Lenox and Tilden Foundations.

102. Noah Webster, p. 119.

103. *Ibid.*, pp. 120-21, 132.

104. Kames, pp. 294-309.

105. Burton MSS. See "Trumbull's Tribute to Humphreys," in Leverett Belknap's *Scrapbook*, III, 18, Connecticut State Library.

106. Frank Landon Humphreys, II, 436.

107. David Humphreys, *The Miscellaneous Works of David*

Humphreys, Esq. late Minister Plenipotentiary to the Court of Madrid (New York, 1804).

108. Review section of *The Monthly Anthology, and Boston Review*, I, 11 (September 1804), 507.

109. *Ibid.*, p. 508.

110. *Ibid.*, pp. 508-9.

111. *Ibid.*, p. 511.

112. *Ibid.*

113. *Journal of the Proceedings of the Society Which Conducts The Monthly Anthology and Boston Review*, ed. M. A. DeWolfe Howe (Boston, 1910), p. 318.

114. Letter from David Humphreys, February 4, 1805, Burton MSS.

115. Lewis P. Simpson, ed., *The Federalist Literary Mind* ([Baton Rouge], 1962), p. 25.

116. "Col. Humphreys' Works," *The Monthly Anthology, and Boston Review*, II, 1 (January 1805), 7.

117. *Ibid.*, p. 9.

118. "Miscellany," *New-England Palladium*, XXV, 11 (February 5, 1805), 1. The other parts were published January 29, February 1, and February 8.

119. *Ibid.*, No. 10 (February 1, 1805), 1.

120. *Ibid.*

121. *Ibid.*

122. Dedicatory letter from Humphreys to Trumbull, August 4, 1790 in Humphreys' *Works* (New York, MDCCXC), p. 117.

123. Letter from Noah Webster to Jedidiah Morse, July 30, 1806 in Warfel, p. 269.

Chapter Seven

1. "*To my good Catechist*," *The Connecticut Journal*, No. 277 (February 5, 1773), p. 1.

Selected Bibliography

PRIMARY SOURCES

1. Books, essays, broadsides

An Essay on the Use and Advantages of the Fine Arts. Delivered at the Public Commencement, in New-Haven. September 12th. 1770. New Haven: T. And S. Green, [1770].

An Elegy, On the Death of Mr. Buckingham St. John, Tutor of Yale College, Who Was Drowned in His Passage from New Haven to Norwalk, May the 5th, 1771, n.p., [1771].

The Progress of Dulness, Part First: Or the Rare Adventures of Tom Brainless. [New Haven: T. and S. Green], 1772; second edition [New Haven: T. and S. Green], 1773.

The Progress of Dulness, Part Second: Or an Essay on the Life and Character of Dick Hairbrain of Finical Memory. [New Haven: T. and S.. Green], 1773.

The Progress of Dulness, Part Third, and Last: Sometimes Called, The Progress of Coquetry, or the Adventures of Miss Harriet Simper. New Haven: Thomas and Samuel Green, 1773.

M'Fingal: A Modern Epic Poem. Canto First, or The Town-Meeting. Philadelphia: William and Thomas Bradford, 1775 [1776].

M'Fingal: A Modern Epic Poem, in Four Cantos. Hartford: Hudson and Goodwin, 1782.

The News-Carrier's Address to His Customers. Hartford: n.p., January 1, 1783.

[The News-Carrier's] Address to the Gentlemen and Ladies that he supplies with the "Freeman's Chronicle." Hartford: n.p., 1784.

Biographical Sketch of the Character of Governor Trumbull. [Hartford: Hudson and Goodwin, 1809].

The Poetical Works of John Trumbull, LL.D. 2 vols. Hartford: Samuel G. Goodrich, 1820.

Address of the Carrier of the "Connecticut Courant," to His Patrons. Hartford: n.p., January 1, 1824.

2. Items in periodicals

"The Meddler," *The Boston Chronicle,* September 4, 1769–January 15, 1770, *passim.*

"The Correspondent," *The Connecticut Journal, and the New-Haven Post-Boy*, February 23—July 6, 1770, *passim;* "To my good Catechist," February 5, 1773; "The Correspondent," February 12—September 3, 1773, *passim.*

"An Elegy on the Times," *The Massachusetts Spy*, September 22, 29, 1774.

"By Thomas Gage . . . A Proclamation," *The Connecticut Courant*, August 7, 14, 1775 (also issued as an eight-page pamphlet: *A New Proclamation.* [Hartford, 1775]).

A letter in support of a copyright law, *The Connecticut Courant*, January 7, 1783.

"The Speech of Proteus to Aristaeus, Containing the Story of Orpheus and Eurydice," "The Downfall of Babylon," "The Prophecy of Balaam," *The American Museum*, July 1787; "Ambition—An Elegy" (more commonly known by the title "On the Vanity of Youthful Expectations. An Elegy." See *Poetical Works* II.), August 1787.

"The Wedding: An Epithalamium," *The Columbian Magazine, or Monthly Miscellany*, June 1789.

"The American," *The Connecticut Courant*, January 7—April 15, 1793, *passim.*

"Mother Carey's Chickens," *Gazette of the United States*, April 13, 1793.

Letter defending *The Miscellaneous Works of Col. Humphreys* in *The Monthly Anthology, and Boston Review*, I, 14 (December 1804); II, 1 (January 1805).

Letter defending *The Miscellaneous Works of Col. Humphreys* in the *New-England Palladium*, January 29, February 1, 5, and 8, 1805.

A letter to C. S. Van Winkle, *The New-York Literary Journal, and Belles-lettres Repository*, III (June 1820).

["To thee, *Dear Nancy*"], *Independent Statesman & Maine Republican*, July 12, 1823.

"Address of the Carrier of the *Connecticut Courant*, to His Patrons," *The Connecticut Courant*, January 4, 1825.

A letter to Samuel Converse, *New-York Evening Post*, March 28, 1826, printed May 17, 1826.

Fourth-of-July address, *Detroit Gazette*, July 11, 1826.

3.   In collaboration

Identified contributions: a treatise called "Prosody" in Noah Webster's *A Grammatical Institute of the English Language, Part II,*

Hartford: Hudson and Goodwin, 1784; and parts of Joel Barlow's *Doctor Watts's Imitation of the Psalms of David, Corrected and Enlarged,* Hartford: Barlow and Babcock, 1785.

Unidentified contributions: Washington's "A Circular Letter . . . to the Governors of the several States," Headquarters, Newburgh, June 8, 1783; parts of "American Antiquities" and related verse, *The New-Haven Gazette, and the Connecticut Magazine,* October 26, 1786–September 13, 1787 (later published as *The Anarchiad: A New England Poem,* written in concert by David Humphreys, Joel Barlow, John Trumbull, and Dr. Lemuel Hopkins, ed. Luther G. Riggs. New Haven: Thomas H. Pease, 1861); the "Prologue" and the "Epilogue" to *The Widow of Malabar* and *The Miscellaneous Works of Colonel Humphreys,* New York: Hodge, Allen, and Campbell, 1790; and "Address from the inhabitants of this City [Hartford], to the President of the United States," *The Connecticut Courant,* August 19, 1793.

4. Manuscripts

The Detroit Public Library and the Cornell University Library have the largest John Trumbull collections. The first words are used for a title when none is given in the manuscript.

a. The Detroit Public Library (Burton Historical Collection, Woodbridge Papers)

Manuscripts of poems. Published: "Epistle to M^r H——" (except the last two lines) and "An Epitaph on Phinehas White, Student of Yale Col." in Alexander Cowie's *John Trumbull: Connecticut Wit*; "Epithalamion Stephani et Hannæ" in *The Columbian Magazine, or Monthly Miscellany* as "The Wedding: An Epithalamium"; "Address of the Carrier of the *Connecticut Courant,* to His Patrons," January 4, 1825; and a fragment (10 lines) of "The Owl and the Sparrow—A Fable" and a fragment (13 lines) of "Advice to Ladies of a Certain Age" printed in *Poetical Works.* Unpublished: "Epitaph To be inscribed on the Marriage Bed of Miss S . . . W . . . ."; [Th]e Village Merchant . . . in the manner of Goldsmith, in his 'Deserted Village' "; "Elegy on the death of a Sheriff; being a Parody on Gray's Elegy in a Country Churchyard"; ["The Muse now mourns in sad, repentant verse"]; and "Hither the worthy," a eulogy.

Manuscripts of prose. Published: "4th of July address by John Trumbull," *Detroit Gazette,* July 11, 1826. Unpublished: four chapters of the fragmentary novel "The Mathematical Metaphysician" and a brief sketch of a continuation; fragments on criticism; "I've seen an end of what we call Perfection here below"; and "To the Committee of correspondence for the County of Wayne, on the part of the Friends of *John Biddle*."

Miscellaneous: Tombstone inscription for David Humphreys, LL.D. [February 21, 1818], written in Latin; and some relevant Trumbull family and other correspondence.

b. The Cornell University Library (Moses Coit Tyler Collection)

Manuscripts of poems. Published: ["Come, Blessed Saviour, quickly come"]; "From a Pastoral"; "Introduction to a satirical poem"; "Poetical Inspiration"; ["And as when Adam met his Eve"]; "Extempore in a dispute, On t[he] Philanthropy of the Author of Tristram Shandy"; ["Join too the hooting Owl in chorus"]; "Part of my first sketch of an Elegy on the death of Mr St. John"; "On the Marriage of Two special Friends of the Author, Mr D. L. and Miss S. C."; "On some Ladies joining to hiss Mr Q.—'s oration at the Commencement at Harvard College"; "Funeral Oration" (except the last two lines) in Alexander Cowie's *John Trumbull: Connecticut Wit*. Fragment of "Ode to Sleep"; first part of "To my Friends, Messrs Dwight & Barlow On the projected publication of their Poems in London" (Lines Addressed to . . . .") in *Poetical Works*. Unpublished: ["While You, my Friend, to flow'ry meads resort"]; ["Mount 'Fancy's Horse' "]; "To a Lady, who made the Author a present of an Embroidered Purse"; "First lines of a Translation of the Beginning of the Poem of Silius Italicus on the Punic War"; ["So some fair towe(r)"]; "The Ring, To two Ladies, who enjoined the Writer to compose a poem on that Subject"; "——'s consolatory verses to his Master, on the loss of his small Clothes, in a Cytheraean Adventure"; "Epigrams"; ["The Bell of night struck one"]; "Perfectability of Man"; two translations from Latin; "[E]pistle [Addres]s[ed] to Mr I. J."; "To a Lady on returning her thimble"; and "Epistle to ———."

Manuscripts of prose. Published: "The Meddler," numbers I, II, V, VII, VIII, and X in *The Boston Chronicle*; "The Correspondent," numbers I, II, IV, V, VI, VII and VIII in *The Connecticut Journal, and the New-Haven Post-Boy*; and "On Romances & Novels" in Cowie's "John Trumbull Glances at Fiction," *American Literature*, XII (1940), 69-73. Unpublished: "1st Sketch of Paper, reviving the *Correspondent*"; "The Cort No ——— By

the Editor of his Works"; "Speculative Essays, On various Subjects"; "Critical Reflections"; "On a Passage in L. Kaims"; "On
Satirical productions"; "Poems on Several Occasions; Part first
. . . Advertisement"; "On Johnson's Imitations of Juvenal's Satires"; notes on literary criticism; background essay preceding
manuscript version of "The Correspondent," Number I; "Extract
to Ja^s A. Hillhouse"; and a draft of the Fourth-of-July address, 1826.

Letters: to John Trumbull from Buckingham St. John on December 4,
1770 and to John Trumbull from John Adams on April 2, 1790.

SECONDARY SOURCES

*American Annual Register of Public Events for the Year 1831-32,
    The.* Brattleboro': Fessenden and Company, 1833. VII, 381-85
    (Appendix). Early account of Trumbull's life; nearly accurate
    in its details.
COGAN, CLARE I. "John Trumbull, Satirist." *The Colonnade,* XIV
    (1919-1922), 79-99. One of the first twentieth-century ap-
    praisals; competently done.
COWIE, ALEXANDER. *John Trumbull: Connecticut Wit.* Chapel Hill:
    University of North Carolina Press, 1936. Indispensable pioneer-
    ing study. Carefully documented and particularly valuable up
    to 1782.
————. "John Trumbull as a Critic of Poetry." *New England
    Quarterly,* XI (December 1938), 773-93. Excellent analysis of
    Trumbull's views on poetry.
————. "John Trumbull as Revolutionist." *American Literature,* III
    (November 1931), 287-95. Disputes the view that Trumbull
    was a fiery patriot.
————. "John Trumbull Glances at Fiction." *American Literature,*
    XII (March 1940), 69-73. Valuable for the essay printed but
    erroneous in stating that Trumbull opposed the novel.
DEXTER, FRANKLIN BOWDITCH. *Biographical Sketches of the Graduates
    of Yale College with Annals of the College History,* III (May
    1763-July 1778). New York: Henry Holt and Company, 1903.
    Essential information about Yale men.
DUYCKINCK, EVERT A., and GEORGE L. DUYCKINCK. *Cyclopaedia of
    American Literature.* New York: Charles Scribner, 1855. De-
    pendable article on Trumbull with long quotations.
GOODRICH, S. G. *Recollections of a Lifetime, or Men and Things
    I Have Seen.* 2 vols. New York: Miller, Orton and Mulligan,
    1857. Slightly inaccurate details about Trumbull by a friend.

GRANGER, BRUCE INGHAM. "Hudibras in the American Revolution." *American Literature*, XXVII, 4 (January 1956), 499-508. Places *M'Fingal* and other Hudibrastic poems into perspective.

————. "John Trumbull and Religion." *American Literature*, XXIII (March 1951), 57-79. Detailed account of Trumbull's attitude toward religion.

GREY, LENNOX. "John Adams and John Trumbull in the 'Boston Cycle,'" *New England Quarterly*, IV (July 1931), 509-14. Presents a strong case against the identification of John Adams as Honorius in *M'Fingal*.

HAZELRIGG, CHARLES TABB. *American Literary Pioneer: A Biographical Study of James A. Hillhouse*. New York: Bookman Associates, 1953. Includes details on Trumbull's advice to James Abraham Hillhouse.

HOWARD, LEON. *The Connecticut Wits*. Chicago: University of Chicago Press, 1943. Readable but undocumented account of Trumbull.

KETTELL, SAMUEL. *Specimens of American Poetry, with Critical and Biographical Notices*. 3 vols. Boston: S. G. Goodrich and Company, 1829. Valuable as an early estimate of Trumbull's worth.

KNAPP, SAMUEL L. *Lectures on American Literature, with Remarks on Some Passages of American History*. [New York]: Elam Bliss, 1829. Another early recognition of Trumbull's contribution to American letters.

LEISY, ERNEST E. "John Trumbull's Indebtedness to Thomas Warton." *Modern Language Notes*, XXXVI (May 1921), 313-14. Points out similarities between Warton's *The Progress of Discontent* (1746) and *The Progress of Dulness*, Part I.

LOSSING, BENSON J. Notes to the 1860 edition of *M'Fingal*. New York: G. Putnam, 1860. Pp. 169-322. Copious notes perceptively written.

MIZE, GEORGE E. "Trumbull's Use of the Epic Formula in *The Progress of Dullness* [sic] and *M'Fingal*." *The Connecticut Review*, IV, 2 (April 1971), 86-90. Presents the epic qualities of both poems; states that they are more in the tradition of the comic epic than the mock epic.

"Original Communications," *The Monthly Magazine, and British Register*. VI, 35 (August 1798), 81-82. Estimate of Trumbull by Elihu Hubbard Smith, an acquaintance.

PARRINGTON, VERNON LOUIS, ed. *The Connecticut Wits*. New York: Harcourt, Brace and Company, 1926. Judicious choice of readings and a generally sound introduction emphasizing socio-economic aspects of the authors' lives and works.

————. *Main Currents in American Thought: An Interpretation of American Literature from the Beginnings to 1920.* Vol. I, *The Colonial Mind.* New York: Harcourt, Brace and Company, 1927, 1930. Includes excellent section on Trumbull's background, political views, and works.

ROTHMAN, IRVING N. "John Trumbull's Parody of Spenser's 'Epithalamion.'" *The Yale University Library Gazette,* XLVII, 4 (April 1973), 193-215. Trumbull's burlesque of epithalamia given in the Yale manuscript reading; three other versions collated with it. A number of factual errors.

SCHORER, CALVIN E. "John Trumbull on Erie's Serpent-Haunted Shore." *Michigan History,* XLII (September 1958), 331-42. Readable description of Trumbull's years in Detroit.

SCHULZ, MAX F. "John Trumbull and Satirical Criticism of Literature." *Modern Language Notes,* LXXIII (February 1958), 85-90. Treats the poet's special interest in satirical criticism.

SHELDON, F[REDERICK]. "The Pleiades of Connecticut." *Atlantic Monthly,* XV (February 1865), 191-92. Condescending appraisal of Trumbull and his associates.

STEDMAN, EDMUND CLARENCE. *Poets of America.* Boston: Houghton, Mifflin and Company, 1885. Sound estimate of Trumbull's place in American literature.

TRUMBULL, J. HAMMOND, ed. *The Memorial History of Hartford County, Connecticut, 1633-1884.* Projected by Clarence F. Jewett. 2 vols. Boston: E. L. Osgood, 1886. Invaluable for background facts on Hartford.

————. *The Origin of M'Fingal.* Morrisania, New York: n.p., 1868. Originally published in *The Historical Magazine* for January 1868. Argues that "By Thomas Gage . . . A Proclamation" was the "origin" of *M'Fingal.*

TRUMBULL, JOHN. *The Satiric Poems of John Trumbull: The Progress of Dulness and M'Fingal.* Edited with preface and notes by Edwin T. Bowden. Austin, Texas: University of Texas Press, 1962. Valuable introduction places the two poems into perspective. Useful for those wanting only Trumbull's two main works.

TURNER, L. D. "John Trumbull's 'The Correspondent,' No. 8." *The Journal of Negro History,* XIV, 4 (October 1929), 380-81, 493-95. Trumbull's satirical attack on slavery is summarized and praised for its effectiveness.

TYLER, MOSES COIT. *The Literary History of the American Revolution, 1763-1783.* Students' ed. 2 vols. New York: G. P. Putnam's Sons, 1897. A standard work.

WOODBRIDGE, WILLIAM. *An Address Before the Detroit Young Men's Society, Delivered by Request, April, 1848.* Detroit: Printed by

Garrett and Geiger, 1849, pp. 22-23. The "Note" at the end
stresses Trumbull's importance as a propagandist for the Revolution; describes the circumstances which led to the composition
of *M'Fingal.*

Index